CHARACTE]

Irene Best, early 40s, brisk and e
Frank Bevan, late 40s, a ladies' ɪ
Rose Macinerny, 19, plump and mousy
Zelda Gregory, late 30s, tall and angular
Dorian Pouvier, late 30s, slim and fair
Rachel Gay, 30s, extremely attractive
Aileen Wheeler, early 20s, a blonde stunner
Caroline Doon, late 30s, tall and well modelled
Inspector David Charlesworth, 30-something,
    boyishly good-looking
Sergeant Lilian Wyler, late 30s, solid and no-nonsense

SYNOPSIS OF SCENES

The action of the play takes place in the back room of Christophe et Cie, a small couture house just off Regent Street, London.

ACT I
SCENE 1 Late August, early Monday morning
SCENE 2 An hour and a half later

ACT II
SCENE 1 Two days later, mid-morning
SCENE 2 The next day, mid-morning
SCENE 3 The next day, late morning

Time — 1937

ACT I

SCENE 1

"Christophe et Cie", just off Regent Street, London. Early Monday morning in late August, 1937

A small couture house of the sort that has almost disappeared. But we are not in the elegant salon, we are in the "backstage" area that the customer never sees

At the rear, up two or three steps, are the double doors that lead into the salon. They are in silver and red plush and offer a glimpse of the quite different world beyond. At either side of this door are stairs leading up to a balcony off which are several offices. Downstage right is an open doorway leading down stairs through to the basement that contains the kitchen and washroom areas and the side entrance. The main area is flanked by archways leading into the staff room and a changing room. There are chairs, a cutting table and a small desk with a telephone, design photographs, ashtrays and a waste bin. A full-length mirror. All the furniture, which includes three stools and a few chairs, is in black and chrome. There are dress and hat display stands, one of them holding a red frock, the others empty. Shelves with material samples. A small selection of shoes   clothes Rail

Irene Best, the senior member of the sales staff, stands by the desk, looking through the morning's mail. She is a small brunette in her early 40s. She is brisk, efficient but insecure and not averse to a little sentimentality. She wears a light summer topcoat over an immaculate but discreetly tailored suit

Frank Bevan comes out of his office. He is the proprietor. A ladies' man of mature good looks, in his late 40s, he has dark hair and the fashionable pencil moustache. He wears a well-tailored double-breasted suit and carries a hat. He uses cigarettes from a silver case

Irene looks up, surprised to see him, as he comes down the stairs

Irene Good-morning, Mr Bevan — I had no idea you were in.
Bevan Good-morning, Irene, pleasant weekend?

Irene Very pleasant, thank you Mr Bevan — and yourself?
Bevan Yes — very pleasant. I'm just popping over to the bank — shouldn't be more than half an hour or so.
Irene Very good, Mr Bevan.

He makes to go downstairs but she can't resist

(*Brightly*) Big day, today.

He looks at her, taking it in

Bevan Yes. Yes it is.
Irene I'm sure that whatever you decide it will be for the best.
Bevan (*after hesitating*) Yes. Yes I'm sure it will. Thank you.

He smiles his charming smile and goes out

She stands for a moment, pleased with their exchange, then resumes looking through the mail, dividing it into two piles

Rose Macinerny dusts her way in through the salon doors, somewhat tunelessly humming a popular song

Rose — known to most as "Macaroni" — is the general factotum. Not yet 20, she is plump and mousy and without makeup. She'd be quite pretty if she lost some weight. Willing but mentally slow. Some might suggest that this slowness conceals a native craftiness. She wears a floral pinafore over her skirt and blouse. She studiously circles the duster over the doors, still humming

Irene Was there nothing from Feldman's?

For a moment Rose does not respond and then

Rose Oh — sorry — pardon?
Irene There should have been a sample from Feldman's.

Rose works it out

Rose Just what's there — sorry.
Irene Not your fault, dear. Put these on Miss Gregory's desk and these on Miss Doon's, there's a good girl.

She holds the piles of mail out for Rose who takes them in both hands

Irene (*of the right hand*) Miss Gregory ... (*of the left hand*) ... Miss Doon — (*and, not heavily*) — and I do wish you'd told me Mr Bevan was in.
Rose I forgot.
Irene Do try to remember things, Rose.
Rose Sorry.
Irene For your own sake, mm?

Rose goes up the stairs and into Gregory's office. Irene takes up her handbag and goes into the staff room. Rose comes out of Gregory's office, moves to Doon's office and goes in

Gregory enters from downstairs. She is the boss's right hand. Late 30s, tall, rather angular, heavily made up and dressed with immaculate care, including gloves and a small handbag. Think Duchess of Windsor. She has cold eyes and is feared by most of the staff

Irene comes back without her topcoat and handbag but with an elegant turquoise blue overall which she puts on and zips up

Gregory checks herself in the full-length mirror

Irene Good-morning, Miss Gregory.
Gregory Good-morning.

Rose comes out of Doon's office but, seeing Gregory, ducks back inside again

Irene Would you like some coffee?
Gregory (*applying a touch more lipstick*) I've just had some — is Mr Bevan in?
Irene He's just gone over to the bank. (*Helpfully*) Mr Pouvier's in — (*indicating*) — in the salon.
Gregory What's he fussing about now?
Irene No, no, he's arranging the window display and ——
Gregory Let me know when Mr Bevan comes back (*She makes to go upstairs to her office*)
Irene (*brightly*) Big day today.

Gregory turns to look at her

Gregory (*knowing perfectly well*) Is it?
Irene Mr Bevan's going to tell us who he's putting in charge of the new salon.

Gregory So he is. As you say, a "big day".

Irene For someone.

Gregory (*with a sarcastic edge*) For you perhaps, Irene.

Irene Oh, I shouldn't think so. I should think it's either you or Miss Doon.

Gregory Should you? Well we'll have to wait and see, won't we? (*She continues to her office*)

She catches Rose trying to sneak out of Doon's office

Rose Good-morning, Miss Gregory.

Gregory Good-morning. (*But*) Have you done something to your hair?

Rose (*patting her hair, flattered*) No.

Gregory No, I thought not — and do take that thing off, this isn't the scullery, you know.

She goes into her office, leaving the door open

Rose comes down the stairs

Rose Should I get her a coffee? (*She sneaks a look at her hair in the mirror*)

Irene She doesn't want one — (*irritably*) — now go and do what she says and get rid of that apron.

Rose Sorry — I forgot I still had it on.

Irene Just do it, please.

Rose The thing is ... I've got a lot on my mind this morning.

Irene We all have, Rose.

Rose No, not about the new shop, it's ... (*she realizes she is saying too much*) ... personal. Sorry. (*She makes to go downstairs*)

Irene And while you're there, check that we're all right for biscuits and so on — Mrs Parkington-Blair was in on Friday and we had nothing to offer her.

Rose I think we might need some sugar.

Irene (*patiently*) Then make a *list*.

Rose Yes, Mrs Best. (*She makes to continue downstairs*)

Irene Rose ... I shouldn't have spoken to you like that. I — um — I got out of the wrong side of the bed this morning. (*She smiles*) Sorry.

Rose's face lights up

Rose That's all right.

Irene And if there *is* anything bothering you, you know where to come, don't you? (*She smiles*)

Rose beams back and goes downstairs. If she had a tail she'd be wagging it

Irene sighs at her own bad-temper and adjusts the red frock on the <u>*stand*</u>

Dorian bustles in from the salon. He is the showroom manager. A slim, fair, self-important man in his late 30s with impatient hands. He wears a lavender grey suit with matching shirt and tie

Dorian (*calling and clapping his hands lightly*) Miss Wheeler!
Irene She's not here, Mr Pouvier.
Dorian (*looking at his wristwatch*) It isn't good enough, you know, it really isn't good enough.

Gregory appears in her office doorway

Gregory What's the problem?
Dorian The problem, Miss Gregory, is that the grey model has got to be finished to take over to Lady Whatsit at the Ritz and I need Miss Wheeler for a final fitting.
Gregory What time is your appointment?
Dorian Two o'clock as it happens.
Gregory Then you've got over four hours. Stop fussing.
Dorian I am not fussing, I ——

Gregory has already gone back into her office, pointedly closing the door

Dorian God, how I dislike that woman. Let me know as soon as Miss Wheeler deigns to put in an appearance. (*He makes to return to the salon*)
Irene Mr Pouvier ... what would you think about putting the red frock in the window? (*She indicates the red frock*) I thought it would look rather tasteful with just the grey hat and a parasol.
Dorian Yes, it probably would, but there's really not much point, is there, because whatever goes in, *she'll* only tell her beloved Bevan that it should have been something else, won't she? (*He makes to return to the salon; aware of Gregory's proximity*) Interfering cat. I wish to God he'd send *her* to the new salon in Deauville, then we'd be free of her.
Irene You think it *will* be her?
Dorian I think it will be whatever *she* wants.

Dorian returns to the salon

Irene stands for a moment, then goes into the alcove and returns with a grey evening frock

Rachel Gay enters from downstairs. She is in her 30s and extremely attractive. A "vendeuse" who started working life as an actress. She is carrying her panama hat and a folded newspaper

Rachel Sorry I'm late, Rene darling, the buses are terrible. And the conductor was in the foulest mood — ringing his bell and sending people flying all over the place. I wouldn't be surprised if they're thinking of going on strike again.

Irene Oh don't say that, Rachel, we've only just got over the last one.

Rachel I had to stand all the way and look what some fool did to my new hat. (*She holds out the hat, showing a mark on it*) Knocked it clean out of my hand. It's going to be one of those days, I know it is.

She goes into the staff room and comes out, putting on her blue overall

Irene Is Aileen with you?

Rachel She's telling Macaroni about the new Clark Gable. Did you have a nice weekend?

Irene Same as usual. Nothing special. And you?

Rachel Oh. You know.

Irene How *are* things?

Rachel Oh Rene, I'm really worried ——

Aileen Wheeler comes in. Aileen is a blonde stunner in her early 20s. A languid goddess much influenced by screen heroines. Streamlined eyebrows, the lot. She drifts rather than walks and affects an upper-class drawl that sometimes slips to reveal her London working-class origins

Aileen Good-morning — or should I say *bonjour*? (*She looks at herself in the mirror, enjoying what she sees*)

Irene moves to push open the salon door

Irene (*calling off*) Aileen's here, Mr Pouvier — (*to Aileen*) — we need you to put this on, dear, quick as you can. (*She holds out the grey frock*)

Aileen Oh not the grey, I hate the grey.
Irene Nevertheless, dear, nevertheless.

Aileen goes into the changing room

Aileen (*off*) Has anyone telephoned for me?
Irene   } (*together*) { Not that I'm aware of.
Rachel   }   { No idea, darling.
Aileen (*off*) He said he'd phone, the swine.
Irene Aileen dear, your language.
Aileen (*off*) Yes, good, isn't it?
Irene And you really shouldn't give people this number.

Dorian comes through

Dorian Where is she?
Aileen (*off; calling*) I'm in here, Dora.
Dorian How many more times? Do not call me Dora.

Aileen comes out in her underwear, high heels and stockings

Aileen Did I say Dora? Sorry, Dora.

Dorian ignores this and helps her into the frock, then moves around her, putting in a pin here, a pin there   PINS

Gregory comes out of her office and down the stairs

Gregory (*of the red frock*) Why is this here?
Irene I — I thought it might look rather good in the window.
Gregory Did you, did you really? (*She continues on her way to the salon*) If Mr Bevan wants me, I'm over in the stockroom trying to sort out the mess that always seems to happen whenever I turn my back for five minutes.
Irene Yes, Miss Gregory.

Gregory goes into the salon

Aileen Good-morning, Miss Gregory. And good-morning to you too, Miss Wheeler.
Dorian Keep still — (*to Irene*) — I told you, didn't I? The woman's a bitch.
Aileen Your language, Dora.
Dorian Keep — still.

Rose comes in and loiters quietly

Irene (*brightly*) Ten o'clock. (*To Rose*) Open up, will you, dear?

Rose obediently goes through into the salon

Dorian Is Miss Doon not in yet?
Irene Yes she is rather late, isn't she?
Aileen Not that she gives a damn whether she's late or not.
Dorian Perhaps Bevan has told her that she's not getting the new job in Deauville and she's sulking.
Rachel She's hardly the sort to sulk, is she? Not Doon.
Dorian (*of the frock*) There — and do be careful.
Aileen Give me a hand, Rache.

Rachel helps Aileen out of the frock

Irene Have *you* been to Deauville, Mr Pouvier?
Dorian Not really, no.
Irene I must say I'd love it if he sent me.
Aileen When I go, I shall be taken, not sent.
Irene Deauville. It sounds so ... French.
Rachel Yes, it would be lovely, wouldn't it? Gaily-coloured umbrellas growing out of flat golden sand ...
Aileen ... the air positively drenched with Chanel Number Five ...
Rachel ... everyone rich and idle and beautifully dressed.
Dorian It's only just across the other side of the Channel, for goodness' sake: it takes longer to get to *Margate*.
Aileen Is that as the crow swims, Dora?
Dorian Nothing's ever serious with you, is it Aileen?
Aileen Not if I can help it.
Rachel You'd love to go, surely Mr Pouvier?
Dorian Whether I would or not, I suspect I'm far too valuable here.

Rachel and Aileen chorus "Ooo". Dorian ignores them

Dorian (*of the frock*) Attend to that as soon as possible, please Irene.
Irene Of course, Mr Pouvier.
Dorian On second thoughts, I'll take it over myself.
Irene Yes, Mr Pouvier.

Dorian moves to the salon door. He holds it open for Rose to come in and goes through into the salon

Aileen Why are you all so concerned about it?
Irene About what, dear?
Rachel Oh come on, Rene — about whom he'll be sending to France.
Irene Because it affects us — all of us.
Aileen It doesn't affect *me*.
Irene Don't be so silly, Aileen.
Aileen Silly nothing. This place isn't the be-all and end-all for *me*, you know. I'm just passing through.
Irene Put a cover on this, please Rose — and very very carefully. (*She gives the frock to Rose, indicating for her to carry it across both arms*)

Rose carries it through into one of the side rooms like it is an unexploded bomb

Rachel (*knowing full well*) Passing through in which direction, darling?
Aileen In the direction of a very rich man who'll do anything for me.
Rachel Oh, nothing's changed then.
Aileen Oh, everything changes. And a lot quicker if you make it change.
Rachel I do believe she means it.
Aileen You betcha bottom dollar I mean it.

It hasn't been a heavy exchange, just Aileen letting the world know — again — where she stands

Aileen goes into the staff room. Rose comes in holding the dress, now under a cover

Rachel I wouldn't mind going, if I'm honest.
Irene Same here, really. Truth is, I'd love it. Thank you, Rose: take it through to Mr Pouvier, will you?

Rose carefully carries the dress through into the salon

Rachel Anyway, as things are for me at the minute, it's out of the question.
Irene No, it'll definitely be between Doon and Gregory.

Aileen returns tying on a long silk robe

Rachel Imagine if he sends Doon — and Gregory is left in sole charge of this place.

Irene Oh God, the thought of it. Gregory would be unbearable.
Rachel That's the thing, isn't it? I mean, Doon might be a bit of a
madam at times, but at least you can talk to her.
Aileen When she's in the mood.
Rachel Yes, she can certainly be — unpredictable. Especially lately.
But Gregory's impossible.
Aileen Well she must have *something* or he wouldn't have had his little
fling with her.
Irene Sshh. We're not supposed to know that.

Irene glances at Rachel: a look we will come to understand later

Aileen Oh come on, Rene. Besides, he's tried it on with all of us, hasn't
he?
Irene He certainly hasn't "tried it on" with *me*.
Aileen You know what I mean, poppet.
Rachel Well whichever one he chooses, he's bound to have trouble with
the other one.
Irene You can't mix business with pleasure.
Aileen What a dear old-fashioned thing you are, Rene.
Rose I think it's Miss Doon.

They all turn to look at her

   Sorry.
Rachel Miss Doon what?
Rose What he's sending to France.
Irene What makes you say that, dear?
Aileen Yes, come on, Macaroni, spill the beans.
Rose You won't say anything?
Rachel Oh do stop being so mysterious, darling.
Rose Well ... when I was polishing his desk, I happened to notice his
diary ——
Aileen Yes, well one does, doesn't one?
Irene Shush, Aileen.

Doon appears in the downstairs doorway No

The others fail to notice, so intent are they on Rose's gossip

*Doon, a New Zealander, is the boss's left hand. In her late 30s, she is
tall, well modelled, every line of her body outlined and emphasized by
her somewhat exotic clothing. Her auburn hair is caught in a twist at the*

nape of her neck. She leans against the doorframe during the following, an amused smile playing on her lips, taking out a cigarette   C͏IGARETTE

Rose It was open, you see. That's how I saw it.
Irene Saw *what*, dear?
Rose That he's taking her out to dinner.
Rachel Taking *who* out to dinner?
Rose Miss Doon.
Irene Tonight?
Rose No — dinner time.
Rachel She means luncheon.
Rose Oh — yes — sorry — lunch. So I suppose they're going to talk about it. The new job.

They take this in for a moment

Aileen You're not as silly as you look, are you, Macaroni?
Rachel Well if she's right, it's certainly going to put Gregory's nose out of joint.
Irene Oh the other hand, he might be taking Doon out to explain why he's giving the position to Gregory.
Doon (*in a New Zealand accent*) "Oh what a tangled web we weave". Is this private gossip or can anyone join in?

They all turn to look at her. Doon lights her cigarette

Irene Good-morning, Miss Doon.

The others ad-lib their "good-mornings". Rachel indicates for Aileen to follow her into the changing room

Aileen follows Rachel into the changing room unhurriedly

Doon perches on the edge of the desk

Doon I take it the boss isn't in.
Irene He has been but he's popped over to the bank — will you excuse me, there's no one in the salon.

It's an obvious excuse to duck this embarrassing situation. She makes for the salon but remembers

Have you made out that list yet, Rose?

Rose (*having of course forgotten*) I was just going to.

Irene If you need some money, Miss Doon will give you some out of the petty cash.

Doon That's me: the keeper of the cash — right, Macaroni? (*She smiles mockingly again*)

Irene, not really understanding, tries a smile back and goes into the salon

Rose tries to sneak downstairs

Doon Bring me up a glass of water, will you?

Rose Yes, Miss Doon. (*She makes to go*)

Doon Quite the little detective, aren't you? (*She "smiles"*)

Rose I didn't mean anything by it.

Doon You might need a better excuse if Mr Bevan were to find out where else your sticky little fingers have been.

Rose (*worried*) You said you wouldn't.

Doon Yes, I did, didn't I? (*She smiles and moves closer to Rose*) But the thing is ... sometimes something happens to make you change your mind — about a lot of things. (*Smiling again*) I'm teasing you, Macaroni ... I'm teasing you.

Is she? Whatever, she pats Rose's cheek and goes upstairs and into her office

Aileen, still wearing the robe, comes out and goes to the desk, sits on the corner showing plenty of leg and dials the phone

Aileen (*lightly*) Cheer up, Macaroni, it's never that bad, I promise you.

Rose snaps out of her thoughts and goes downstairs without acknowledging Aileen

Perhaps it is.

Irene comes in

Irene You really shouldn't be using the telephone you know, Aileen.

Aileen Would you prefer me to shout out of the window?

Irene You know what I mean. (*Quietly*) What if Miss Gregory should catch you?

Aileen Miss Gregory isn't here, is she?

Irene Yes, but —
Aileen Anyway, he isn't answering, the stinker. (*She replaces the receiver*)

Unseen by them, Doon comes out of her office and stands looking down at them, smoking

Aileen Men. Why is it you can never trust them an inch?
Irene (*primly*) I've no idea I'm sure.
Doon What are you two gassing about?
Aileen Irene was telling me about her love life.
Irene I was doing no such thing.
Aileen (*to Doon*) You know what they say — it's always the quiet ones.
Irene Stop it, Aileen, you're embarrassing me.
Doon (*suddenly sharp*) Be quiet, the pair of you. I've got a headache and you're making it worse.

Irene shoots a look at Aileen: now look what you've done

Doon Where's Macaroni?
Aileen She's just gone downstairs.
Doon I asked her to bring me up a glass of water.

Dorian puts his head round the salon door

Dorian I'm back.
Irene Thank you, Mr Pouvier.
Doon Morning, Dora.
Dorian (*stiffly*) Good-morning, Miss Doon.
Doon Busy weekend?
Dorian Not particularly, thank you.
Doon You didn't "pop down" to the seaside then — for some fresh air and fun.
Dorian As it happens, I visited my mother who, I have to tell you, is not at all well.
Irene I'm sorry to hear that, Mr Pouvier.
Dorian She has heart trouble.
Irene Oh dear.
Dorian Not serious — but enough for concern.
Doon You'd better make sure she doesn't get upset then, hadn't you? But then you're a very considerate son, I'm sure. Your sort usually is. (*She "smiles"; to Irene*) See what's happened to my glass of water, will you?

Doon goes into her office

Dorian realizes that the others are looking at him and goes through into the salon

Irene What was that all about?
Aileen (*unconcerned*) No idea, darling. She's obviously in one of her bitchy moods.
Irene His mother doesn't live at the seaside, she lives in Croydon.
Aileen Poor cow.
Irene What's that girl doing with her glass of water, it can't be that difficult, surely? (*She makes to go downstairs*)

The telephone rings

Aileen I'll go.

Aileen strolls across and downstairs

Irene answers the telephone

Irene Christophe, Irene Best speaking, how may I help you? ... Oh yes, good-morning Mrs Courtney-Hope. Yes he is indeed. One moment, I'll fetch him for you. (*She goes to the salon door*) Telephone call, Mr Pouvier.

Rose comes in, carrying a glass of water and goes to Doon's office, concentrating hard on not spilling any. After a moment, we see Doon close the door

Dorian bustles through from the salon

Dorian Who is it?
Irene Mrs Courtney-Hope. (*She holds the receiver out to him*)

Dorian rolls his eyes and takes the receiver

During the following, Rose comes out of Doon's office and discreetly goes downstairs. Aileen comes in and perches on the desk, examining her nails

Dorian Good-morning, Mrs Courtney-Hope, Dorian Pouvier speaking. And how was Biarritz? (*Pause*) Did you, did you really? That sounds absolutely divine, I'm so jealous. The new peacock silk? ... Oh I do agree, it would suit your delicate colouring perfectly. Yes. Yes. When would you be able to come in? ... I shall put it in my appointments book and very much look forward to seeing you. In the meantime I shall have a few drawings prepared for you to look at. ... Yes. Yes. Bye. (*He hangs up*) "Nothing elaborate, Monsieur Pouvier, just cut quite plain with a vee neck, you know I don't like naked shoulders". Nor do I, you great lump, not if they're the size yours are. A vee neck. Can you imagine?

He shudders and goes back into the salon

Rachel comes in, holding her straw hat

Rachel What am I going to do about this blasted hat?
Aileen Don't ask me, poppet.
Irene Let me see. (*She takes the hat and holds it up to the light*)
Irene Try oxalic acid. (*She hands back the hat*)
Rachel Oxalic what?
Irene Acid, oxalic acid. There was an article about it in *Good Housekeeping*. It comes in sort of crystals — like salt. You just rub it in and then brush it off again. It's supposed to be marvellous. It does brass and everything.
Rachel Where do I get it?
Irene The chemist across the road should have some. Take the hat over at lunch-time and show him.
Rachel Mm. I might pop over now, while it's quiet.
Aileen It'll be quiet all day.
Irene Why not send Rose?
Rachel Because, knowing Rose, she's likely to get it all wrong and come back with a bottle of syrup of figs.
Aileen My father swears by syrup of figs. "Look after your bowels, my girl, and your bowels will look after *you*."
Rachel Charming.

She takes off the overall as she goes into the changing room

Aileen How's your kid, by the way?

Rachel comes out, with her jacket, and looks at Aileen suspiciously

Rachel Why do you ask?
Aileen Just wondered how he was.
Rachel He's — he's very well, thank you.
Aileen How old is he now?

Rachel He's six. (*To Irene*) I won't be long.
Irene What if Mr Bevan comes in? Or Gregory?
Rachel You'll think of something, Rene darling, I know you will.
Irene That is so unfair, Rachel.
Aileen Everything's unfair in this world, Rene — that's why you have to look after number one.
Irene Well ... be quick.
Rachel (*taking up the hat*) How much should I get?
Irene (*edgily*) I don't know — ask the chemist.
Rachel Don't *worry*, darling.

She gives Irene a peck on the cheek and goes downstairs

Aileen You really are twitchy today, aren't you, Rene?
Irene Yes, but ... what if a customer comes in?
Aileen Sweetie — there's nobody here, they're all out of town, it's that time of year. God, it must be wonderful to be able to say that. "Out of town".
Irene Well Mrs Verner's coming in this morning, I know that for a fact.
Aileen And probably the only customer we'll see all day. All week I shouldn't wonder. Just think: I could be on someone's yacht somewhere. Which reminds me. (*She takes up the telephone and dials*)
Irene I really wish you wouldn't do that.
Aileen I know you do, poppet. (*She blows her a kiss and continues dialling*) I want him to collect something for me and he's bound to forget.

Irene takes the red frock from the stand

(*Listening on the phone*) Is Rachel worried about her kid?
Irene Not that I'm aware of.
Aileen Not still having trouble with that awful husband of hers, is she?

Before Irene can answer, Gregory comes in from the salon. She sees Aileen using the telephone

Gregory Is that a private call?
Aileen I don't know, Miss Gregory. (*She unhurriedly replaces the receiver*)
Gregory What d'you mean, you don't know?
Aileen I mean it was for you but they rang off. (*She smiles sweetly*)

At the sound of Gregory's voice, Doon comes out of her office, cigarette in hand, and stands looking down

Gregory I understand from the stockroom that you "borrowed" the new chiffon last week.
Aileen (*pretending to think back*) Yes. Yes, I think I did.
Gregory And that it was torn when you returned it.
Aileen Was it? No one said.
Gregory Who gave you permission to take it?
Doon I did.

They look up at her

Gregory The stockroom is *my* responsibility.
Doon So you keep telling us.
Gregory Then why wasn't I informed?
Doon I dunno. Maybe you were out somewhere, gallivanting around on your high horse. (*She blows out smoke insolently*)
Gregory I wonder if Mr Bevan would find your attitude quite so amusing.
Doon Why don't we ask him?
Gregory Yes, why don't we?

A moment between the two of them. Then Gregory moves to her office

If I were given charge of this place there'd be a great many changes, I can promise you.

She goes into her office, closing the door

Aileen Thanks.
Doon I didn't do it for you. But next time — ask.
Irene How's your headache, Miss Doon?
Doon What? Oh — yes — better, thank you.

She goes into her office

Irene Oh Aileen, you're so irresponsible.
Aileen I borrowed a dress, for God's sake.
Irene And tore it.
Aileen Oh shut up, Rene, you're like the Mother Bloody Superior.
Irene Language!
Aileen Knickers!

Rachel comes in from downstairs. She holds up a small paper bag, twisted closed

Rachel Here I am, you see ... no time at all.

She gives Aileen the hat and goes into the changing room

(*Off*) Did anyone say anything?
Aileen Not a sausage, sweetheart.

Rachel returns with her overall that she puts on as Aileen tries on the hat

How do I look?
Rachel Like a million dollars, darling.

Aileen admires herself in the mirror

Aileen I'll give you ten bob for it.
Rachel Some hopes.
Irene (*of the bag*) How much did you get?
Rachel He said an ounce should be ample.
Aileen Let's have a look. (*She takes the bag and starts to untwist it*)
Rachel Be careful — it's poison.
Aileen (*"impressed"*) Is it really? (*She licks a finger and pretends to put it into the bag*)
Irene Don't be so silly, Aileen!
Aileen I'm teasing. Believe me, I have no desire to kill myself. There's far too much in the offing.
Rachel And far too many doing the offering.
Aileen Well well, get *you*.
Rachel Sorry darling, couldn't resist.
Aileen Oh you must resist, darling ... or at least until you get what you want.
Rachel Do you ever *listen* to yourself, Aileen?
Aileen Good God, no, sweetie, I might give myself the wrong idea.

Rose comes in from downstairs

Rose Excuse me.
Irene Yes dear.
Rose I'm just going to give the receipt to Miss Doon. (*She holds up a piece of paper. What a good girl am I*)

Loose charge

Irene Oh, you've been — thank you, Rose.
Rose And the change.

*She holds up a palmful of small change and goes upstairs, knocks and
goes into Doon's office*

Rachel She nearly got herself killed just now, you know.
Irene She what?
Rachel I was coming out of the chemist's when I saw her crossing the
road towards the little grocer's on the corner — she walked straight
out, in a complete dream, almost under a taxi — what he called her I
really couldn't repeat.
Aileen Oh go on.
Rachel I asked her if she was all right and she just stared at me as
though I were Boris Karloff or someone.

Rose comes out of Doon's office and down the stairs

Irene (*brightly*) All right, Rose?
Rose Yes, thank you, Mrs Best.

She goes downstairs without looking at anyone

Irene She's such a sweet girl but, I don't know, she gets more of a
liability every day. I'm beginning to wonder how long we can keep
her on. In fact ... well don't say anything, but I heard Gregory talking
to Mr Bevan about her.
Aileen Oh don't say she's trying to get her the sack.
Irene Well, knowing Gregory.
Aileen Poor little cow. No family and not two ha'pennies to rub together.
(*She takes off the hat and gives it to Rachel*)
Rachel Times aren't easy for *anyone*, darling.
Aileen No but they're a damn sight easier for some than others.
Rachel (*to Irene*) So what do I do with this stuff?
Irene You just brush it on and rub it off.
Rachel Right.
Irene You're not going to do it now, are you?
Rachel Oh, Rene.
Irene Well then ... I wouldn't use all of it — see how it goes.

A buzzer sounds briefly and a light flashes by the salon doors

Irene (*to Aileen*) There you are, you see — a customer.

Irene goes briskly into the salon

Rachel What I need I suppose is a brush of some sort.
Aileen (*taking up the telephone to dial*) There's an old toothbrush of mine in the cupboard downstairs.
Rachel Thank you, darling.

Rachel goes downstairs

Irene comes in quickly and goes to call down the stairs

Irene Rose!
Rose (*off*) Yes, Mrs Best?
Irene A cup of coffee, dear — on a tray.
Rose (*off*) Yes, Mrs Best.

Irene collects three or four dresses

Aileen Who is it?
Irene Never seen her before. She's American — a Mrs Herbert Fischbaum.
Aileen (*not seriously*) Ask her if she knows Clark Gable.

But Irene is already on her way into the salon

Rachel comes in from downstairs, with the toothbrush

She sees Gregory coming out of her office and pockets the toothbrush and busies herself tidying the display stand Irene just used. Gregory comes down the stairs, and looks through the material samples

Aileen (*idly, back to her nails again*) Have *you* seen the new Clark Gable, Miss Gregory?
Gregory No I have not.
Aileen I saw it Saturday. Cocktails ... then the flicks — best seats in the new Odeon in Leicester Square — then supper at the Café Royal.
Gregory Isn't that where your mother is a waitress? How very embarrassing for you. Oh no, begging her pardon, she works at Lyons Corner House, doesn't she? What is it they call the waitresses there? Nippies. That's it, Nippies. Very hard work, I should imagine. Still: hard work but happy work — and who wouldn't be happy, knowing one's station in life and not trying to be something that one isn't.

Irene comes back in with the dresses and holds one out for Aileen

Irene This one, dear.

Irene gives the dress to Aileen and hurries back into the salon

Gregory takes some material samples up to her office   Material
                                                           Samples

Aileen takes off the dressing gown and puts on the dress

Rachel (*of Gregory*) What a bitch that woman is.
Aileen Oh she'll get her comeuppance one of these days, don't you
worry — give me a hand with this, will you, Rache.

Rachel helps Aileen with the dress   Tray, cup, milk
                                                         jug, sugar bowl
*Rose, wearing the apron, comes up with a tray holding a coffee cup,
milk jug etc. She moves towards the salon as though she's carrying a
saucer of nitro-glycerine*

Irene comes through from the salon

Irene Are you ready, Aileen?
Rachel Two ticks. (*She collects appropriate shoes from their selection
and gives them to Aileen*)
Irene (*to Rose*) I'll take that, shall I, dear?
Rose Thanks ever so much.
Irene (*whispering*) Apron, dear, apron.

Irene takes the tray and goes back into the salon

Rose makes to go back downstairs

Aileen Remember what I told you, Macaroni.

Rose looks at her

Rose I forget.
Aileen You're as good as anyone. *Anyone*.

Rose takes it in, nods and continues downstairs

Rachel There — off you go.

Aileen takes a look at herself in the mirror and goes into the salon

Rachel remembers the brush in her pocket, collects the hat, opens the packet of crystals on the desk, puts the waste bin on the desk, tips a little of the crystals on to the hat stain and starts tentatively brushing at it, over the wastebin

Doon comes out of her office, holding a ten shilling note. She comes down the stairs and across to call

Doon Macaroni!

Rose hurries upstairs

Rose (*anxiously*) Yes, Miss Doon?
Doon Fetch me some cigarettes, will you? (*She holds out the note*)
Rose (*relieved*) Yes, Miss Doon.

Rose takes the note and goes out

Doon What's that you're doing?
Rachel Well it's very quiet this morning so I thought I'd have a go at getting this mark off my hat.
Doon (*of the packet*) What's this stuff?
Rachel Oxalyic acid crystals — it's supposed to be very good.
Doon Acid? Shouldn't you be wearing gloves or something?
Rachel Apparently it's only dangerous if you swallow some.

Doon watches her working on the hat for a moment

Doon Have you ever thought about killing yourself?
Rachel (*making it light*) Don't say that.
Doon We've all got to die. It's having the courage to say when.
Rachel Courage?
Doon I think so.
Rachel What a horrid conversation for this time of a morning.
Doon You're right. Sing us a song.
Rachel (*smiling*) Which one would you like?
Doon How about ... "Counting the Days".

Rachel's face changes

Rachel I ... don't know that one.
Doon Really? I thought it would have been your favourite.

Aileen comes in from the salon and gets out of the dress

Rachel helps Aileen, clearly disturbed by Doon's remarks

Dorian comes in, pausing at the door

Dorian I couldn't agree more, Mrs Fischbaum, I couldn't agree more. (*He closes the door*) What a dreadful woman.
Doon Is she buying?
Dorian Yes of course she's buying, she's an American.
Aileen I love Americans.
Dorian "Perhaps you'd like to try something on," I said. (*In a terrible American accent*) "Under no circumstances," she said, "do I take off my clothing in public." "Madam," I said, "If you've got something I've never seen, I'll shoot it."
Rachel You didn't say that.
Dorian No, but I was sorely tempted. (*He collects some design photographs*)

Album of design Photos

Aileen Have you ever been to America, Dora?
Dorian As it happens, I have great chums in Greenwich Village.
Doon Which do you prefer, Dora ... Greenwich Village or Brighton?
Dorian Why do you ——

Dorian looks really upset. But then he shakes his head and goes back into the salon with the photographs

Rachel Brighton?
Doon Our little joke.
Aileen *He* didn't seem to think so.
Rachel (*thinking of herself*) No.

Rose comes in with a packet of cigarettes and coins. She gives them to Doon and goes out again

Pkt cigarettes / Coins

Aileen puts on her robe. Rachel puts the frock on a hanger and Doon sits on the edge of the desk, unwrapping her cigarettes

Irene comes in with her order book

Order book

Irene She's taking three.
Doon *He'll* be happy.

Irene sits at the desk to make out the order slip

Irene Yes, things have been rather slow lately, I must say.

Rachel Makes one wonder why he's opening a new branch. No disrespect, Miss Doon.
Doon He got a good offer and he's taking a risk.
Rachel I should think it is a risk with all that's going on.
Irene What, you mean those awful Germans?
Rachel Have you read what he says, this Hitler?
Irene Well he's mad, obviously. Would you sign this please, Miss Doon?

Doon countersigns the order

Rachel World domination. I ask you.
Irene Oh, Mr Chamberlain will put him in his place. Thank you.

Irene takes the order book into the salon

Aileen Besides, what would Hitler want with a dress shop in Deauville?
Rachel There you go again, always making a joke of things.
Doon You and me both, it seems, Aileen.

Gregory comes down the stairs without anyone else noticing

Gregory Have you got nothing better to do?
Aileen Not really.
Gregory What's this?
Rachel As it's so quiet, I thought I'd try to clean my new hat. I dropped it, you see, and ——
Gregory (*referring to the crystals*) Is this what I think it is?
Rachel It's ——
Gregory You brought it *here*?
Rachel Well as a matter of fact ——
Gregory Have you spilled any?
Rachel No — none.
Gregory Yes you have, there's some in this waste bin.
Rachel Well hardly enough to ——
Gregory I really don't believe you people.

Doon sits to one side, lighting yet another cigarette, enjoying the goings-on

Rachel Well there really isn't anything to do, Miss Gregory.
Gregory Then find something.
Aileen I know: let's play Murder. Who would we like to be the victim?
Gregory You really are a very insolent young woman.
Aileen And what's more I don't know my place. What a hussy I am.

Dorian comes in from the salon, feeling rather pleased with himself.
But his expression soon changes

Gregory Did you know about this, Mr Pouvier?
Dorian Know about what?
Gregory Bringing this dangerous stuff into the establishment.
Rachel It's only dangerous if ——
Gregory Well, Mr Pouvier?
Dorian I've no idea what you're talking about — and besides, I've been
with a client all morning — I can hardly be expected to ——
Gregory Miss Macinerny! (*Generally*) I shall tell Mr Bevan exactly
what goes on when he's not here.
Doon Tell him what you like, you stupid cow. You're a pain in the arse
and I for one am sick of the sight of you. Luckily I won't have to look
at you or your arse for much longer.

Irene, carrying the tray, comes in from the salon and catches the end
of this   Tray

Doon screws out her cigarette and goes up to her office

Gregory remains standing, furious

Irene (*whispering to Rachel*) What's happening?

Rachel mimes for her not to say anything

Rose comes up in her apron

During the following, Dorian whispers to Aileen, asking her what's
going on and she whispers back

Rose Yes, miss?
Gregory Take this downstairs and get rid of it.
Rachel Excuse me.
Gregory Get rid of it.
                                                          Paper bag
                                                          of Chyobals
A moment, then Rachel holds out the packet for Rose who takes it

Rose What is it?
Gregory It doesn't matter what it is, just get rid of it.
Rose How?
Dorian Just ... flush it down the huh-hah.
Rose What, in the paper?

Dorian Oh for goodness' sake ... just flush it away.

Rose looks at the packet and makes to go

Irene Take this down, will you, dear? (*She holds out the tray*)

> *Rose puts the packet in her apron pocket in order to take the tray and goes out*

> *Gregory stands for a moment and then moves up the stairs to her office*

> *Bevan comes in from the salon, wearing his hat. He takes it off as he speaks*

Bevan Why is no one in the salon?
Dorian I was just on my way, Mr Bevan.

He quickly goes into the salon

Irene An American lady we don't know bought three of the little silk two-pieces, Mr Bevan — she said she would most certainly be recommending us.
Bevan (*flatly*) Good.
Gregory Might I have a word with you, Mr Bevan?
Bevan Just one moment, Zelda.
Gregory (*sotto voce*) It's very important, Frank.
Bevan (*sotto voce*) Yes I'm sure, Zelda, but in a moment and please don't use my name during working hours. (*To Irene*) Ask Miss Doon to come and see me, will you please, Irene?

Bevan goes upstairs and into his office

Irene goes up to Doon's office, knocks briefly, puts her head in and comes down again

The buzzer sounds and the light flashes

Rachel I'll go.

Rachel goes into the salon

Doon comes out of her office and goes into Bevan's

Rachel hurries back in and checks through dresses on the rack

Gregory Who is it?
Rachel Mrs Verner.
Gregory Good, I need to speak to her.

Gregory goes into the salon

Rachel finds the dress she wants and holds it up for Aileen who takes it. Show
Irene helps her into it and again sorts out suitable shoes   on Shelf

   Rose comes in from downstairs

Rose Excuse me ... the kitchen boy's here for the dinner order.
Irene (*irritably*) Lunch, Rose, lunch.
Aileen What is it?
Rose Curried rabbit.
Rachel Oh God.
Aileen I'll have yours.
Rachel Oh no you won't — just a small portion for me.
Aileen What's the sweet?
Rose Spotted Dick.
Rachel Oh God.
Aileen Extra custard, please.
Irene Off you go.

   Aileen goes into the salon

Rachel No pudding for me, thank you, Macaroni.
Rose So that's eight dinners and seven puddings. (*She's quite pleased
   with herself at working this out*)
Irene No, no, Rose, not everyone will be here.

   Gregory comes in from the salon

You'll be here for lunch, won't you, Miss Gregory?
Gregory What is it?
Rose }
Aileen } (*together*) Curried rabbit.
Gregory What are the vegetables?
Rose Potatoes and carrots.
Gregory I'll have rice.
Rose Rice.
Gregory Rice, just rice — and no dessert.
Rose So that's eight dinners and *six* puddings.

Irene No, no, Rose.

Rose Sorry.

Irene There'll be six of us — that's right, six — Miss Doon is lunching with Mr Bevan.

Gregory (*sharply*) Who said so?

Rose It was in his diary.

Gregory What are you talking about, in his diary?

Rose No, I was just saying.

Irene (*changing the subject*) So you can tell him six, Rose.

Rose Six dinners and six puddings.

Irene Six lunches, one with rice and *four* sweets, And do put them in the hot cupboards, Rose, last week they were stone cold half the time.

Rose goes downstairs, repeating the order under her breath

Aileen comes in from the salon

Irene helps her out of the dress

Doon comes out of Bevan's office

Doon (*from the balcony, to Gregory*) He wants to see you.

Gregory Actually ... I want to see *him*.

She looks around smugly and goes upstairs. There is a moment between her and Doon before she goes into Bevan's office

Doon drifts down the stairs

Irene I am correct in thinking you'll be lunching with Mr Bevan, aren't I, Miss Doon?

Doon No you're not.

Irene Oh. I thought ——

Doon Well you thought wrong.

Irene So he's ... lunching alone then?

Doon No. He's lunching with Miss Gregory.

Doon goes up and into her office

Irene I wonder what's made him change his mind?

Aileen Who knows, darling? Who knows? (*Unconcerned, she takes up the telephone and starts to dial*)

Irene makes to complain but gives up and goes downstairs

The Lights fade as we bring up the sound of a dance band playing a jolly hit of the moment

The music fades and the Lights come up on the next scene

SCENE 2

The same. An hour and a half later

plates
Jug water
glasses
Newpaper

The cutting table has been set up to eat off. It holds a jug of water and some glasses. Aileen and Irene sit together, on stools. Rachel sits, slightly apart, reading the "News Chronicle". Dorian sits at the end, dabbing his mouth with his coloured handkerchief

Rose comes out of Doon's office and down the stairs carrying an empty tray

wooden Tray

Irene Take these, will you, dear?

Rose collects up the plates. Aileen is quick to help her

No, don't take them all, dear, take the others later.

Rose carries her loaded tray across and downstairs

Aileen stands and wanders around a bit

Aileen D'you know, I'm still hungry.
Rachel How can you still be hungry?
Aileen I don't know, darling. But I am.
Rachel I wouldn't mind if you put any weight on.
Aileen I know, it must be a pain.
Rachel It's unfair, I know that.
Aileen You never put weight on either, do you, Dora? I suppose it's all that walking round Leicester Square you do.
Dorian I really do get sick and tired of these remarks. Why don't you leave me alone?
Aileen (*realizing that she's perhaps gone too far*) You're right. I'm sorry.
Dorian I just get fed up with it, that's all.

Rose comes up with the tray

Aileen helps her reload it

Aileen You fancy coming to that new milk bar tonight, Macaroni?
Rose Me?
Aileen It's amazing. Really American. Come on, I'll buy you a nice strawberry milkshake.
Rose Well, I'm not sure.
Aileen Come on, it'll do you good.

Bevan comes out of his office, carrying his hat. He comes downstairs

Bevan Where's Miss Gregory?
Irene She's powdering her nose, Mr Bevan.
Bevan I'll wait for her in the salon.
Irene I'll tell her.

He makes to go into the salon

Bevan I — er — I know you're all anxious to hear what I have in mind about your future here and I apologize if I appear to be somewhat — tardy — in letting you know exactly what's happening. I was in fact intending to let you know this morning, but due to — er — unforeseen circumstances, I'm afraid you'll have to wait until later this afternoon. In the meantime I want to assure you that none of you has anything to fear as far as your positions are concerned. As long as Christophe remains open, you will remain with it.

He nods, smiles, and goes through into the salon

Irene (*calling after him*) Thank you, Mr Bevan.
Rose (*anxiously*) Does that mean me as well?
Aileen Of course it does.

Rose, relieved, sets about tidying up

Dorian You'll notice he said "as long as Christophe remains open."
Rachel Yes? So?
Dorian So it gives him a little get-out, doesn't it?
Irene I'm sure he didn't mean that at all.
Doon Nevertheless ... it might be as well to start casting one's net.
Aileen Do you know something we don't know, Dor —— Mr Pouvier?
Dorian (*smugly*) Not at all. Not at all.

*Gregory comes through from downstairs with her small handbag
under her arm and a pair of gloves*

Irene Mr Bevan is waiting for you in the salon.
Gregory (*stiffly*) Thank you. (*She pulls on her gloves*)
Aileen Have a nice lunch, Miss Gregory.
Gregory I'm sure I shall, thank you. (*She drops a glove*)

Rose, nearby, picks it up for her

Thank you.

She takes the glove and goes out to the salon

Rachel Well she doesn't look very happy about it.
Rose Her hand was shaking.
Irene Her what, dear?
Rose When I gave her her glove. Her hand was shaking.
Aileen Perhaps she's having a nervous breakdown. Wouldn't that be
wonderful?
Irene Don't be so cruel, Aileen.
Aileen Come on, Macaroni.

*Aileen takes the water jug and glasses and goes downstairs followed
by Rose carrying the loaded tray*

Aileen Anyone fancy a coffee?

The others ad-lib in the negative. Dorian looks at his watch

Dorian I must be going.
Irene Oh yes, you're seeing Lady Sudbroke.
Dorian And dreading it, I can assure you.

He goes into one of the rooms

Rachel He really does make a fuss about everything, doesn't he?
Irene Yes, but he's very kind. (*She sits next to Rachel. Confidentially*)
Is everything going all right with the — you know.
Rachel Another three months and I get my decree nisi.
Irene You must be counting the days.

Rachel looks at her sharply

Rachel Counting the days. Yes.

Irene Once it's all over you'll be so much happier. Free to start your life over again.

Rachel Unless anything goes wrong.

Irene What can go wrong?

Rachel (*after a moment, working into it*) Bobby stayed with his father this weekend. Apparently he was asking questions — my husband.

Irene What sort of questions?

Rachel Oh, just — whether I went out at night — had he ever seen me with anyone — did anyone telephone me — a six-year-old boy being interrogated by his own father.

Irene That's awful.

Rachel It's what happens, Rene: people fall out of love and it becomes so ... so nasty.

Irene But you're not ——

Rachel Of course I'm not. I haven't so much as — passed the time of day with a man. Except ——

Irene Oh Rachel, you were so silly.

Rachel Nothing happened, I swear. But if my husband found out, they're bound to make something out of it.

Irene But he won't find out, will he? I mean, who knows about it, apart from me? And I would never say a word, you know I wouldn't.

Rachel (*putting her hand on Irene's*) I'm sorry to have involved you, truly I am, Rene. But I had to tell *someone*, I was in such a state.

Irene I know, I know. So. Just you and I then.

Rachel And him of course. And ... and I think he might have told Doon.

Irene Surely not. I mean he might be a ... you know ... but he wouldn't do that, surely?

Rachel I don't know. It's the way she looks at me sometimes. And the remarks she makes.

Irene You're probably reading too much into things. You know what she's like when she's in one of her funny moods. Just ignore her.

Rachel Yes, but the thing is ... (*Whatever she was going to say, she decides against. A moment*) I can't let anything go wrong, Rene. If I lost my son ... I couldn't bear it, I just couldn't bear it.

Aileen comes through from downstairs, finishing a biscuit and holding a mug of coffee

Aileen What's up with you two?

Rachel (*brightly*) Oh nothing ... just having a moan.

Aileen takes a look at Rachel's newspaper   Edward/Mrs Simpson

Aileen (*sarcastically*) Oh look, they're on the front page again. (*Reading*) "The Duke and Duchess of Windsor, recently returned from their honeymoon in Austria blah blah blah."

Irene I despise that woman.

Rachel It's all *her* fault, of course.

Irene Yes, well whether it is or not, look what they've done to the poor King. Have you ever seen anyone look so unhappy?

Aileen (*of the newspaper*) Nice frock, though.

Rachel Yes, she dresses well: one can't take that away from her.

Irene But then so does he, doesn't he? Always has.

Aileen Must be wonderful: nothing to do but try on new clothes.

Rachel Yes, I wonder what they'll *do*.

Irene That's not fair: he's very concerned about what's happening, I'm sure he is ... look ... they're going to see Mr Hitler.

Aileen (*reading*) "Plans are being made for the couple to meet Herr Hitler in Berlin where they will study social conditions and housing problems and attend a concert given by the Nazi district orchestra."

Irene There you are, you see.

Aileen I'm surprised they didn't invite Mosley: they could have sat around comparing notes.

Irene Sometimes, Aileen, I just don't understand what you're talking about.

Aileen Anyway. My father says it's not Hitler we should be worrying about, it's the Russians.

Irene I thought you said your father was a communist.

Aileen Socialist.

Rachel Isn't it the same thing?

Aileen Go to Spain, Rache, and you'll find out.

Irene Is your brother still in Spain?

Aileen Yes. Yes he is.

Rachel You must be really worried.

Aileen If you really want to know, I'm worried sick about him. Signing up to fight someone else's war, the stupid bugger.

Rachel You're such a strange mixture, Aileen.

Aileen Perhaps I should have been called Dolly then. Yes, I rather like that: (*she strikes a pose*) Dolly Mixture — star of stage, screen and whatever else she turns her mind to. (*She goes into her rendition of a Jessie Matthews song*)

Irene tries to shush her

Dorian comes in, putting on his jacket

Aileen grabs him and whirls him around. He protests. Suddenly Doon gives a loud cry from her office, which brings everything to a halt

They all turn and look up to see Doon coming out of her office, staggering, clutching at her throat

Rose comes from downstairs to stand in the doorway

Doon tries to say something but can't. Dorian goes quickly upstairs to catch her as she falls. He kneels over her

Irene Is she all right?

A moment. Dorian looks at them

Dorian No, she's not. She's dead.

This moment. Then Rachel slowly sits, staring ahead, and the others remaining looking towards Dorian and Doon

Dance band music plays

CURTAIN

ACT II

Scene 1

The same, two days later, mid-morning

Chairs and stools have been loosely arranged: Aileen, Gregory, Irene and Rachel are sitting. Bevan and Dorian stand. Everyone is dressed differently from when we last saw them. Bevan wears a black tie. Rachel and Bevan are smoking cigarettes. Also present, standing, quietly conferring, are Inspector David Charlesworth and Sergeant Lilian Wyler. Charlesworth is a boyishly good-looking 30-something. Unmarried, he has a deceptively casual manner. He wears a well-cut three-piece double-breasted suit and is holding a trilby hat. Wyler is in her late 30s. A solid, no-nonsense woman but not butch. She wears an off-the-peg tweed suit and flat shoes. She is no fan of the world in which she presently finds herself and does little to hide the fact. She will take notes throughout. Notebook-black

Rose hurries in from downstairs

Rose Sorry.
Charlesworth Not at all.

Rose sits

Rose I wasn't sure I'd turned it off.
Charlesworth Very sensible of you to check. (*He smiles*)

Wyler clears her throat pointedly. Charlesworth puts down his hat

Good-morning — again — ladies and gentlemen ... my name is Charlesworth, Inspector David Charlesworth of the Criminal Investigation Department ——
Aileen And good-morning again to you, Inspector. (*She clearly likes the look of him and has sussed out immediately that she can wrongfoot him with her sort of teasing*)
Charlesworth Good-morning, yes ... and this is my associate, Sergeant Lilian Wyler. We have been called in — as I'm sure Mr Bevan will

already have told you — to investigate the sudden death of Miss Caroline Doon.

Dorian Excuse me.

Charlesworth Yes, Mr —

Dorian — Pouvier, Dorian Pouvier.

Wyler (*making a note*) Pouvier.

Dorian (*correcting her pronunciation*) Pouvier.

Charlesworth Yes, Mr Pouvier?

Dorian You're not suggesting that there are ... suspicious circumstances, are you, Inspector?

Charlesworth Please bear with me, Mr Pouvier.

Aileen *I'll* bear with you — absolutely. And do please make a note of my name — Aileen, Aileen Wheeler. That's A for Available —

Irene Shush, Aileen.

Bevan Yes, may we get on, please? These are very sad circumstances but I must point out that I still have a business to run. We've already been closed for two days.

Charlesworth Indeed, Mr Bevan. But if you'll bear with me I'm sure we shall soon have the sign turned round on your door. (*He smiles. An edge or what? A moment, and he continues*) The post-mortem has shown that Miss Doon was poisoned.

A reaction from them all

Bevan Poisoned?

Charlesworth I'm afraid so. Traces of oxalic acid were found and were almost certainly ingested with her last meal. Which I believe was taken on these premises.

Rachel Oh my God.

Bevan You're surely not suggesting that any of us had anything to do with it?

Charlesworth At the moment I'm simply —

Bevan Good God, it just doesn't happen. Not in a place like this.

Wyler can't resist a little "huh"

Charlesworth I'm afraid death occurs in all manner of places, Mr Bevan. And for all manner of reasons. We know that in this case death was not natural. So that what we have to determine is whether it was accidental, self-inflicted ... or by another's hand.

Dorian Are you saying she was murdered?

Charlesworth I'm saying it's a possibility, Mr Pouvier.

Reaction from the others

Bevan But why would anyone want to kill Miss Doon?
Charlesworth At the moment, I've no idea, Mr Bevan — but, as I
   say —
Rachel Excuse me. I'd like to say something.
Wyler Your name, please?
Rachel Gay, Mrs Rachel Gay.
Charlesworth Yes, Mrs Gay.
Rachel It was my fault. My ... my stupid hat.
Charlesworth Hat?
Aileen It wasn't your fault, Rache.
Rachel Of course it was. If I hadn't bought the stuff —   (*She trails
   off*)
Charlesworth Would you like to explain, Mrs Gay?

Rachel can only shake her head, a handkerchief to her mouth. Aileen ꞁ ɑ n ᴋₑ
comforts her

Irene Excuse me — Mrs Best, Mrs Irene Best.
Charlesworth Yes, Mrs Best?
Irene Mrs Gay was anxious to remove a stain from her new straw hat.
   At my suggestion she bought some oxalic acid crystals.
Charlesworth At your suggestion?
Irene I'd seen an article in one of my magazines. It was ... it was
   supposed to be very good.
Charlesworth And this was when?
Rachel (*bravely recovered*) All right, Rene, thank you ... that same
   morning.
Wyler When you say you bought it, do you mean you brought it here
   with you that morning or —
Rachel No. I went out from here at about what — half-past ten — and
   bought it at the chemist's in Argyll Street.
Bevan Did you, did you really?
Rachel I'm so sorry, Mr Bevan.
Charlesworth That would be Stockwell's.
Rachel Mr Stockwell, yes.
Charlesworth And he gave it to you without question.
Wyler There's no restriction on oxalic acid.
Rachel And he did know me. I go in there quite often for odds and ends.
   I think we all do.
Charlesworth Did Miss Doon know you'd brought it here?
Rachel Yes. She saw me cleaning the hat.

Charlesworth And she knew what you were using.
Rachel I — I told her.
Charlesworth Who else knew the acid was on the premises?

Hands go up with varying degrees of enthusiasm

All of you, then.
Bevan I didn't actually see the stuff but I was told about it by Miss
Gregory.
Aileen I bet you were.
Wyler (*writing*) Gregory.
Gregory (*putting her hand up a little*) I'm Miss Gregory. Zelda.
Wyler (*writing*) Z-E ——
Gregory (*impatiently*) Z-E-L-D-A —— It's not that difficult, surely?
Dorian Excuse me ... I only knew about the hat and everything when I
was told by Miss Wheeler. I never actually ... *saw* anything.
Charlesworth Thank you, Mr Pouvier.
Wyler How much did you buy, Mrs Best?
Rachel I think he said an ounce. Yes, an ounce. About four teaspoonsful.
Wyler And did you use all of it on the hat?
Rachel No, I used about half. Yes, about half.
Charlesworth What happened to the rest?
Rachel It was — thrown away.
Charlesworth How d'you mean, thrown away?
Gregory I can answer that.
Charlesworth Yes, Miss Gregory.
Gregory I saw what Mrs Gay was doing and with what, and told her to
get rid of it.
Charlesworth You knew it was potentially dangerous.
Gregory I'd seen it used before — I can't remember where.
Charlesworth And so you got rid of it.
Rachel Yes.
Charlesworth How?
Dorian At my suggestion it was thrown down the huh-hah.
Charlesworth I beg your pardon?
Wyler The lavatory.
Charlesworth Ah, the lavatory. The lavatory being?
Irene (*pointing*) Downstairs. In the basement.
Charlesworth And that's where it was disposed of.
Gregory (*irritably*) Yes.
Charlesworth By you, Mr Pouvier?
Dorian Certainly not. By Miss Macinerny.
Wyler Miss Macinerny.

Rose Pardon?
Charlesworth You disposed of the acid crystals.

Rose doesn't understand quite what he means

Dorian You put the crystals into the lavatory.
Rose (*after a moment*) Yes.
Charlesworth And flushed them away.
Rose (*after another small moment*) Yes.
Wyler Did anyone see you do it?
Gregory Yes. I did.

Rose looks hugely relieved

Rose Yes. Miss Gregory.
Charlesworth Thank you.
Wyler Is that M-A-C or M small c?
Rose Pardon? Oh ... Rose Agnes Macinerny ... (*she studiously spells out her surname*) ... Miss.
Gregory Oh, for God's sake.
Rose Sorry.
Aileen No need to apologize, Macaroni.
Wyler Macaroni?
Aileen Macinerny, Macaroni.
Rose It's a thingy, a whatsit, a nickname.
Wyler I see.
Gregory So childish.
Charlesworth I'd like to move on, if I may, to lunch-time. Is the food prepared here or brought in?
Bevan It's brought in. Not only here but to the girls in the workshop.
Charlesworth Brought in from where?
Bevan From Lorenzo's — the restaurant in Maddox Street.
Charlesworth So how does it work?
Bevan A boy comes over and takes the order — how many lunches are required, are there any special requests, the usual sort of thing.
Charlesworth What time would that be?
Bevan I've no idea.
Gregory Usually around eleven o'clock.
Charlesworth So that's what would have happened on this particular morning.
Gregory Yes, exactly that.
Charlesworth And the food is delivered at —— ?
Irene A quarter to one. Sometimes a little earlier, but never later.

Wyler What happens to it? Is it served straightaway or what?

Irene No, it's kept warm in the hot cupboards, downstairs in the kitchen.

Charlesworth And then you serve yourselves.

Gregory Some of us are served — the more senior staff — the others collect their trays for themselves.

Charlesworth Served by?

Gregory Miss Macinerny.

Rose Sorry? Oh — yes.

Charlesworth Were you all here for lunch that day?

Bevan No. Miss Gregory and I were lunching at the Savoy.

Charlesworth But you were here when the food was delivered.

Gregory Yes.

Charlesworth So it's safe for me to say, is it, that as well as Miss Macinerny, each of you could have had access to the food in the period between it being delivered and being served.

Dorian I don't like the implication, but yes we could.

Wyler Did Miss Doon help herself or was she served?

Irene She was served. By Miss Macinerny. That's right, isn't it, Rose?

Rose Pardon? Yes. I took it up to her office on a tray. (*She indicates*)

Charlesworth So she ate alone.

Irene She did, yes.

Charlesworth Was that usual? For her to eat alone?

Irene It really depended.

Charlesworth On what?

Aileen On what sort of mood she was in.

Charlesworth Can you ... explain that a little further?

Rachel I don't wish to speak ill of the dead but Miss Doon had what you might call a very changeable personality.

Charlesworth Changeable.

Rachel Unpredictable.

Aileen One never knew quite where one was with her. (*To Gregory, smiling*) Did one?

Rachel Especially the last month or so.

Dorian To be honest, if she chose, she could be something of a bitch.

Irene Language, Mr Pouvier.

Dorian I'm sorry, but there we are.

Charlesworth (*after a moment*) Well ... thank you for your time, ladies and gentlemen ... now that you've given me a general picture of what happened that morning, I'd like to speak to each of you individually ——

Bevan There's nothing more we can tell you, surely?

Charlesworth Let me be the judge of that, if I may, Mr Bevan ... so ...
if I may ask you all to perhaps wait in the showroom, we'll call you in
as we need you. If I may start with you, Mr Bevan.
Bevan (*irritably*) Yes, yes, yes.

*The others go through into the salon, some whispering to others, some
not, Aileen giving Charlesworth a flighty smile*

Charlesworth (*when they have gone*) Let's, er, let's have some chairs,
shall we, Sergeant?

Wyler moves three chairs so that they form a little group

Is there a "Christophe"?
Bevan My father. Christopher actually. He died some years ago. Now
look here, Inspector, I do hope there's not going to be a lot of publicity
about this — unfortunate affair. I've seen the harm it can do and
frankly, at this particular time, I don't need it.
Charlesworth It very much depends on the press. If they want to plug
it, I'm afraid there's very little we can do to stop them. However, if the
death shows itself to be accidental, I can't see them —
Bevan Of course it was an accident — which wouldn't have happened
if that damned woman hadn't brought the stuff into the place.
Charlesworth No. (*He smiles; indicating*) Please sit down, Mr Bevan.

They sit. Wyler slightly to one side as she takes her notes

Tell me about Miss Doon.
Bevan She — came to this country from New Zealand. I don't know
why, I never asked. A couple of years ago she answered an advertise-
ment for a sales assistant but it soon became clear that she was much
too valuable to be left in that kind of post and so I promoted her to
being my design consultant. She has — had — a very good eye.
Charlesworth Did that cause any resentment?
Bevan I employ mostly women, Inspector. There was bound to be some
tongue-wagging, women — (*to Wyler*) — if you'll excuse me — being
women. And you know what they say about this business.
Charlesworth I'm afraid I don't.
Bevan Stitch and Bitch, Inspector.
Charlesworth Ah. Yes. Quite. Stitch and Bitch. (*He smiles*)
Wyler (*writing*) "Stitch and Bitch."

Charlesworth holds his smile but drops it suddenly

Charlesworth But you can think of no particular reason why anyone should hold a grudge against her?
Bevan (*after a slight moment*) No.
Charlesworth Or why she should take her own life?
Bevan None at all. But then I only knew her in a — business capacity. Quite what went on in her private life, I can't say.
Wyler You didn't know any of her acquaintances?
Bevan No.
Wyler Or meet her outside of business hours?
Bevan Once or twice perhaps. For the odd drink. But nothing of any significance.
Charlesworth Well thank you, Mr Bevan. You've been most helpful. I wonder if you'd be kind enough to send in ... (*he looks at Wyler's notes*) ... Mrs Best.
Bevan Of course. (*He makes to go*) Inspector ... you must forgive me if I at first seemed somewhat — irritable. I know you have your work to do but the truth is I'm extremely upset by this affair and I ... well I'm sure you understand.
Charlesworth Indeed. Oh — by the way — are you married, Mr Bevan?
Bevan No. No I'm not. Although frankly I don't see what that has got to do with anything.
Charlesworth No. (*He smiles, offering no further explanation*)

Bevan hesitates a moment, then nods and goes through into the salon

Wyler Upset? Him? Only about how much money he's losing. And decidedly shifty in my not very humble.
Charlesworth A ladies' man surrounded by ladies.
Wyler A ladies' man with all the cards in his hand.
Charlesworth Worth a few enquiries, I would have thought, Lilian.
Wyler (*indicating her pad*) Already in the book.

The salon door opens and Irene puts her head round and comes in

Charlesworth Ah. Mrs Best. Do sit down.

She sits and can't help fidgeting with the corner of her jacket, her nervousness very apparent. Charlesworth remains standing

Tell me something about your work here.
Irene I'm the senior member of the sales staff. I've been at Christophe's since before old Mr Bevan died ... (*but she can't resist*) ... this is terrible, terrible. I can't sleep thinking about it.

Charlesworth Perhaps you'd prefer to continue this later, Mrs Best?
Irene No, no, I'm all right. Thank you. If my poor dear husband were alive, it might be different, I could have had someone to lean on, but he died five years ago. He was a bird-fancier, you know. A harmless enough hobby you would have thought but one of them pecked him on the nose and he died of blood poisoning. You just don't know what's round the corner, do you?

Charlesworth decides it might be better for Wyler to take over. He indicates so to her

Wyler How did you feel about Miss Doon?
Irene I liked her. Most of the time.
Wyler Most of the time.
Irene I really don't want to speak ill of the — you know.
Charlesworth I'm afraid ... (*He shrugs his apology at the unavoidable*)
Irene Well ... she could be quite difficult in view of her up one minute down the next personality. I put it down to her being a colonial but Rachel — Mrs Gay — says it's because of her artistic nature. Apparently artists are like that. I myself was brought up in a cathedral city and find that sort of thing rather self-indulgent.
Wyler Did the others find her difficult?
Irene Like me really. Basically we liked her but we had to be careful. Not Aileen — Miss Wheeler — she really, well, she doesn't seem to worry about anything —and Miss Gregory, of course.
Wyler Miss Gregory?
Irene She and Miss Doon didn't hit it off at all. She's very close to Mr Bevan, you see, his right hand man you might say, and when Miss Doon came along and became his well, favourite, the atmosphere here changed rather.
Wyler So there was a rivalry between them.
Irene Yes, but only in trying to impress Mr Bevan. I imagine that's why he decided to send one of them to Deauville.
Charlesworth How d'you mean, Mrs Best?
Irene He's opening a new branch in Deauville — you know, in France — and about two weeks ago told us that one of us would be sent there as general manager. We were terribly excited, of course. Well — general manager — France — a new start in a new country. The day — the day poor Miss Doon died, we found out it was to be Miss Gregory.
Charlesworth And how did Miss Doon react to that?
Irene Well that was the thing.

They wait for her to continue. She doesn't

Wyler What was?
Irene Well ... she seemed — well, quite indifferent.
Charlesworth Not jealous — or distraught.
Irene Not in the slightest. Which I must say surprised me.
Charlesworth And how did you feel? About not getting the job?
Irene Oh, I was never really in the running. I would have loved it, of
course, but no ... my place is here I think. Well I know it is.
Charlesworth (*after a moment, standing*) Well, thank you, Mrs Best
... I wonder if you'd be good enough to send in ... (*he checks Wyler's
book*) ... Mr Pouvier.

Irene hesitates a moment, then goes through into the salon

(*Sitting*) What d'you think?
Wyler Can't see it, myself.
Charlesworth Bottom of the list, would you say?
Wyler Always assuming a list needs making.

Dorian comes in

Charlesworth Ah — Mr Pouvier — do sit down.

Dorian sits, pinching the creases of his trousers

Dorian Before we go any further — and since this is a police investiga-
tion — I must tell you that Pouvier is not my shall we say real name.
Charlesworth Ah.
Wyler Your real name being?
Dorian Prout.
Wyler Prout.
Dorian P-R-O-U-T — Prout.
Wyler (*writing*) Dorian ... Prout.
Dorian Derek.
Wyler Derek.
Dorian Yes.
Wyler (*writing*) Derek ... Prout.
Dorian I would be grateful if that information were kept between
ourselves.
Charlesworth Of course, Mr Pouvier.
Dorian (*relieved but trying not to show it*) Thank you.
Charlesworth How long have you been employed here, Mr Pouvier?

Dorian Four years. I'm in charge of the salon and I deal personally with our more influential clientele.

Charlesworth I take it you weren't fond of Miss Doon.

Dorian Not particularly.

Charlesworth In fact you said, she could be ... what was it?

Wyler Something of a bitch.

Dorian Well she was a bitch.

Charlesworth In what way?

Dorian Oh, always trying to put people down ... never missing the chance to make a hurtful remark. Particularly at my expense. Snipe snipe snipe. Does that mean I killed her? No of course it doesn't. Did she kill herself? I've no idea.

Charlesworth Was it always like that with her?

Dorian Was she always so spiteful, you mean? Oh, it wasn't so bad at the beginning, in fact I rather liked her. But this past month or so, she seemed to take a particular delight in ... well, as I've said.

Charlesworth So I imagine you were hoping it was she who would get the job in France.

Dorian Oh, you know about that, do you? Well, to be frank, if anyone was going I rather hoped it would be Gregory.

Charlesworth Oh? Why is that?

Dorian Because she really *is* a bitch. And that's not just my opinion, everyone dislikes her intensely. Ask them.

Wyler Did that include Miss Doon?

Dorian Oh God yes, they hated the sight of each other. Not that I'm suggesting that Gregory had anything to do with what happened. After all, it was *she* who was to be in charge of the new salon, not Doon. That must have given her *enormous* satisfaction. Not that you would have thought so, but then I suppose she was just trying to keep the smirk off her face. (*He can hardly keep the smirk off his own as he flicks away imaginary dust from his trousers*)

Charlesworth Well thank you, Mr Pouvier.

Dorian (*somewhat disappointed*) Is that all?

Charlesworth For the moment. Would you mind sending in ... (*He looks to Wyler*)

Wyler Mrs Gay.

Charlesworth Mrs Gay, please.

Dorian As you wish.

Dorian goes into the salon

Wyler He wasn't wrong, was he? Bevan? "Stitch and bitch."

Charlesworth (*grinning*) "Mirror mirror on the wall, who is the bitchiest of them all?"

Wyler Mind you, you should hear some of our lot in the canteen. "A woman detective? Next thing you know they'll be promoting one of the *horses*."
Charlesworth It's a man's world, Lilian.
Wyler Not in here it isn't.

Rachel comes in

Charlesworth Do sit down, Mrs Gay.

She does, nervously. He sits

Tell me about yourself.
Rachel Well ... I'm a *vendeuse* ... a sales lady ... I've been here for just over two years ... I'm married ... well, in the process of a rather nasty divorce ... and I have a son. (*Wretchedly*) If only I hadn't dropped my stupid hat ... if only I hadn't rushed round to the chemist and not waited 'til lunch-time ... but that's so often what life's all about, isn't it? "If only". (*This moment. She looks on the point of tears, but recovers*) I'm so sorry. Please ask your questions: I'll tell you whatever I can.
Charlesworth How did you get on with Miss Doon?
Rachel I liked her. She could be — tricky — you know — unpredictable and sometimes quite cruel — but mostly she was ... fun.
Charlesworth Did you ever see her socially?
Rachel No. Never.
Charlesworth Do you ever socialize with any of the staff?
Rachel Not really, no.
Wyler Or Mr Bevan?
Rachel (*too quickly*) No. No, never.

They let this hang in the air a bit

Charlesworth I understand that Miss Doon had a rather difficult relationship with Miss Gregory.
Rachel Who told you that? Dora I suppose.
Wyler Dora?
Rachel I beg his pardon — Mr Pouvier.
Charlesworth (*smiling*) That's what you call him, is it — Dora?
Rachel I think it was Aileen — Miss Wheeler — who started it and I sort of — picked it up. What was it you asked? Oh yes — Gregory. No, they didn't really get on. There was a great deal of rivalry. Mainly on Gregory's side, I think. Doon seemed to take pleasure in — egging her on. Which was very typical of her. There was a sort of — devil in her at times.

Charlesworth Devil?
Rachel She would provoke — atmospheres. Setting one person against the other. At first it was — well, quite amusing to be honest — but she seemed to get more and more malicious. It was as though she was... punishing us for something. I came to the conclusion that there was something disturbing her, something she couldn't come to terms with and was, well, lashing out at others instead. (*She realizes and makes light of it*) I suppose that sounds like a load of mumbo-jumbo. The sort of stuff actors seize on when they're searching for motivation.
Charlesworth Policemen too, Mrs Gay. (*He smiles*)
Rachel Yes. Yes of course. (*She returns his smile, relaxing a little*)

A moment

Charlesworth When you cleaned the hat ... you said you did it over a waste bin.
Rachel Yes — there — on the desk — to catch any of the crystals I might drop.
Charlesworth And did you? Drop any?
Rachel A little — yes.
Charlesworth And you left it in the bin.
Rachel No — I took it downstairs and tipped it into the toilet.
Wyler Seems to have been quite busy, that toilet.
Charlesworth Did anyone see you do it?
Rachel (*after a slight hesitation*) No. But I can assure you that that's what happened.

A moment. Charlesworth smiles

Charlesworth You know, Mrs Gay ... I'm sure I've seen you before. Is that possible?
Rachel I've no idea. Unless you go to the theatre.
Charlesworth Of course! The Hampstead Players. *Darkness Be My Friend* ... *The Lady From The West* ... you were wonderful.
Rachel A long time ago now, I'm afraid.
Charlesworth And you — what — gave it up.
Rachel My husband was rather — jealous of my career.
Charlesworth Then he deprived a great many of a great deal of pleasure.

Wyler sighs heavily and rolls her eyes

(*Standing*) Thank you, Mrs Gay, that's all for the moment.
Wyler Aileen Wheeler.

Charlesworth Would you ask Miss Wheeler to come through, please?

Rachel stands and makes to go

Rachel There is one thing ... when Miss Doon saw me cleaning the hat, she said to me ... "Have you ever thought about killing yourself", and how much courage it would take to do it.
Charlesworth And you think she was serious.
Rachel I'm not sure, it ... it was such an odd thing to say and just in that moment she looked quite — well, yes, serious. Although she quickly laughed it off but then that was her way.
Charlesworth (*nodding*) Thank you.

Rachel remains a moment and then goes into the salon

I knew I'd seen her before. She really was rather good. I seem to remember falling in love with her. I also seem to remember the "if only" speech. I think it was *The Woman In Question*.
Wyler The main thing to remember, I would have thought, is that she's an actress and capable of putting on a performance. Notice how quick she was to tell us about the hat and buying the crystals. Poor me, it's all my fault. And all that "have you ever thought about killing yourself" stuff.
Charlesworth It was Mrs Best who suggested using the crystals, remember.
Wyler Yes, well, I'd keep my eye on her.
Charlesworth We'll keep our eye on all of them, Lilian.

Aileen comes in

Miss Wheeler.

She swans down and, uninvited, sits, crossing her legs, then uncrossing them and sitting demurely

Aileen Before you start, I have a confession to make.
Charlesworth Oh?
Aileen Yes. I have a real thing about policemen. I would have preferred it if you were in uniform, but suspects can't be choosers, can they? Anyway, if you'd like to put the handcuffs on I'll go quietly ... (*She holds out crossed wrists*) Oh dear, I've made you blush. Sexton Blake never blushes, does he?

Wyler clears her throat, indicating to Charlesworth that she'll do the questioning

Wyler What is your position here, Miss Wheeler?

Aileen Usually upright, parading around half-naked.

Wyler (*dour*) You're a model.

Aileen Mannequin. I wear the frocks to show the customers what they'll look like. Or think they'll look like. There are usually two of us but Judy — Miss Cameron — has been off for three weeks with some sort of chest infection.

Wyler How did you get on with Miss Doon?

Aileen Fine. But then I get on with everybody. And if I don't I don't bother with them. That's what I'm always saying to Dora: turn the other cheek, dear.

Charlesworth Miss Doon gave him a bad time, I understand.

Aileen Not always. But she could be very sarcastic with him. I suppose where she comes from his sort are few and far between. They're all so loud and manly in Australia, aren't they, even the women.

Wyler New Zealand.

Aileen (*knowing full well*) Same thing, isn't it? Mind you, some of the things she said, I couldn't make head or tail of.

Wyler Like what?

Aileen Well, like the morning she died, for example ... which do you prefer, Dora, she said ... Greenwich Village or Brighton? — I ask you, what's that supposed to mean? He looked so angry I thought he was going to attack her. Am I being awfully indiscreet or incredibly helpful?

Charlesworth Oh, incredibly helpful. (*He smiles, momentarily forgetting himself. Recovering*) Sergeant?

Wyler Do you think she could have killed herself?

Aileen Not in a million years.

Wyler Why?

Aileen Because she had too much life in her. (*She suddenly looks as if her indifferent façade is in danger of collapsing. She stands, twisting to look down*) Is this seam straight? No I thought not ... (*She puts her foot up on the chair and adjusts her stocking with her back to them, aware that it is discomforting Charlesworth*) Has anyone told you what we had for lunch?

Wyler They didn't have to: it was in the pathologist's report.

Aileen Well if you're going to poison someone, you couldn't do better than serve curried rabbit, could you? My God, the taste of that would drown anything.

Charlesworth You think she was murdered then, do you Miss Wheeler?

Aileen I've no idea, darling, but it does seem awfully convenient, don't you think? (*Referring to the stocking*) That's better, isn't it?

Charlesworth (*lightly*) Who would your money be on then, Miss Wheeler?

Aileen (*taking up the lightness*) Oh, I don't know: to kill someone you'd need a motive, wouldn't you?

Charlesworth Ah — you *have* been reading your Sexton Blakes.

Aileen So the only one I can see who might have a motive is the boss.

Charlesworth Mr Bevan? And why's that?

Aileen Because if you play around on your own doorstep, you're asking for trouble. Why they fall for it, I don't know. Mind you, he's an attractive bastard and he knows it. Oops, language. (*She puts a hand over her mouth*)

Charlesworth (*standing*) Well thank you, Miss Wheeler, you've been very er ——

Wyler Entertaining.

Charlesworth Helpful. Would you mind sending in ——

Wyler Miss Gregory.

Aileen Oh, you'll enjoy that — Miss Gregory is *very* entertaining. Do feel free to interrogate me whenever you feel the urge, won't you, Inspector?

Aileen goes out, giving him a little wave at the door

Wyler Not exactly heartbroken, is she?

Charlesworth Difficult to know *what* she is.

Wyler I would have thought it was obvious.

Charlesworth Too obvious, perhaps?

Gregory comes in

Miss Gregory. Do sit down.

Gregory does so, making it quite clear that she considers herself above all this

(*Smiling*) You're Mr Bevan's "right hand man" then.

Gregory He does put a great deal of trust in me, yes.

Charlesworth Which is why he was putting the new salon in your hands.

The slightest moment

Gregory Yes.

Charlesworth Are you pleased about that?

Gregory Naturally. (*She's clearly giving away as little as possible*)

Charlesworth You were lunching with Mr Bevan that day.

Gregory At the Savoy, yes.

Charlesworth Does that mean you weren't here when the food was brought in?

Gregory No it does not. We were late leaving because Mr Bevan had to take a telephone call. And yes, I went downstairs. To powder my nose.

Charlesworth It must have been a shock when you came back from luncheon and found out what had happened.

Gregory Of course.

Charlesworth Am I right in suggesting that you and Miss Doon were not particularly fond of each other?

Gregory I didn't like the woman, no.

Charlesworth Any — particular reason?

Gregory She was unreliable and far too pushy. Luckily Mr Bevan could see through her.

Charlesworth Oh. I was given to understand that he thought a great deal of her.

Gregory Then you were misinformed.

Charlesworth He — expressed his misgivings to you, did he?

Gregory As I said — he places a great deal of trust in me.

Charlesworth Yes, he made that quite clear.

A white lie that gets the satisfied response he expected: this is a woman to flatter

Gregory He's very appreciative of my loyalty. I know that.

Charlesworth (*sitting*) Confidentially ... are the others as loyal, would you say?

Gregory I wouldn't have thought so: other than Mrs Best.

Charlesworth But she wasn't considered for the job in France.

Gregory Obviously not.

Charlesworth Why obviously?

Gregory Because she has no personality. In a position like that, one needs to have presence and a great deal of charm. Poor Mrs Best, loyal though she is, has neither of those things.

Charlesworth What's your opinion of the others? Between ourselves. (*He leans forward as though very interested in her opinions*)

Gregory Mr Pouvier is good at what he does but makes far too much fuss. I've heard that he has ideas about opening his own salon should he find someone fool enough to provide financial backing. Mrs Gay is efficient enough but sees everything as a drama with herself centre stage — not surprising, I suppose, in view of her previous occupation. Miss Wheeler is as shallow as a side plate. Where she gets that accent from, I've no idea, it fools no one and simply goes to show how common she really is. Miss Macinerny is, I'm afraid, rather simple and makes mistake after mistake. I doubt that she'll be here much longer.

Charlesworth Thank you. That's very useful, Miss Gregory.

Gregory Is that all?

Charlesworth I think so ... (*but*) ... oh — you said you'd seen oxalic acid used before.

Gregory Yes, I knew you'd ask me that. It was my landlady. To remove a stain on a carpet.

Charlesworth Do you think Miss Doon might have killed herself?

Gregory considers uneasily

Gregory I'm quite sure ... I'm quite sure it was some ghastly accident.

A moment. Then Charlesworth nods

Charlesworth Well I think that's everyone, Sergeant.

Wyler Miss Macinerny.

Charlesworth Of course — Miss Macinerny. (*He stands*) Would you be good enough to ask her to come through, Miss Gregory?

Gregory stands and makes to go

Charlesworth Oh — Miss Gregory ... if there's ever anything you think I ought to know ... in confidence of course.

After a moment, Gregory goes through into the salon

Wyler There's a madam and no mistake.

Charlesworth Easy to see why the others don't like her.

Wyler You certainly gave her some flannel.

Charlesworth Yes, and didn't she appreciate it.

Rose comes in

Ah — Miss Macinerny. (*He indicates for her to move in*)

She does so and stands nervously

Do sit down.

She looks at the chair and takes a moment to sit. Charlesworth sits

How old are you, Rose? It is Rose, isn't it?
Rose Yes — Rose Agnes. Nineteen. Well nearly nineteen. October the twelfth.
Charlesworth And how long have you been working here?
Rose Three months. Nearly. Yes, three months.
Charlesworth Do you like your work?
Rose Yes, it's very nice.
Charlesworth How do you get on with everyone?
Rose I don't really have much to do with them. I'm mostly downstairs.
Charlesworth Tell me again what you did with the crystals.
Rose The what? Oh — yes — I put them down the thingy like Mr Pouvier said.
Wyler All of it?
Rose Pardon?
Wyler (*"patiently"*) You're quite sure it all went down the lavatory.

A brief moment. You can almost see Rose's brain working

Rose Yes.
Wyler How can you be sure?
Rose Because it was still in the paper.
Wyler Did you tip it out before you flushed it away or leave it in the paper?

Rose works it out

Rose I put the stuff in first and then I tore the bag up in little pieces and put that in as well.
Wyler Very efficient of you.
Charlesworth And Miss Gregory would have seen you do it anyway.

Rose looks at him, working it out

Rose Yes.
Charlesworth (*smiling*) You took Miss Doon's luncheon up to her office.
Rose First I went up and asked her if she wanted any.
Charlesworth How d'you mean?
Rose Well, we thought she was going out to dinner — lunch — with Mr Bevan, but when we found out she wasn't, Mrs Gay said I ought to ask her if she wanted any so I went up and she said what is it and I told her and she said bring it up with a glass of water so I did.
Charlesworth How did she seem? When you spoke to her?
Rose I don't understand — sorry.

Charlesworth Did she seem in any way upset?
Rose No. She had her feet up on the desk, smoking a cigarette and reading
Vogue. She smoked ever such a lot. Sometimes I fetched her two packets
a day. She let me keep the cards and I give 'em to my brother.

A moment

Charlesworth Well that's all, thank you, Rose.
Rose Shall I go back in with the others or downstairs?
Charlesworth Back with the others.

Rose nods, stands and moves towards the salon

Rose You wouldn't like a cup of tea or anything?
Charlesworth (*smiling*) Not at the moment, thank you.

   Rose nods and goes into the salon

   Not the fastest little filly out of the gate.
Wyler Some of the slowest people I've met have been the most
cunning.
Charlesworth Indeed. So then, where are we?
Wyler If it was an accident it means that somehow the stuff got into her
food and her food alone and I just don't see it.
Charlesworth No, I agree. Suicide?
Wyler Why put it into the food? Why not just swallow it or drink it
down with some water?
Charlesworth But then she did talk to Mrs Gay about killing herself.
Wyler (*from her notes*) "Have you ever thought about killing yourself."
Not quite the same thing I would have thought. And only Mrs Gay's
word for it.
Charlesworth Which leaves us with murder.
Wyler I think so.
Charlesworth So then ... means ... opportunity ... and motive. Who
had what?
Wyler Everyone knew the stuff was here in the building.
Charlesworth And had the opportunity to mix it with the food.
Wyler But only if there was some to mix — that is, the acid that wasn't
used wasn't flushed away.
Charlesworth Exactly. Which would mean that either Mrs Gay — or the
girl ——
Wyler Or both of them.
Charlesworth Or both of them — aren't telling the truth.
Wyler Or Mrs Gay bought more of the stuff than she said she did.

Charlesworth Or someone else brought some of it into the building. A lot of "ors", Sergeant.

Wyler And too many coincidences, wouldn't you say, sir?

Charlesworth If it *was* murder, then it had to be unpremeditated. As Bevan said ... "none of this would have happened if the stuff hadn't been brought here". The hat, the acid, the curry ... I think all these things came together by pure chance and, together with something that happened here that morning, pushed someone over the edge. Someone who had presumably been harbouring something for a long time.

Wyler Which brings us to number three. Motive.

Charlesworth What are the usual? Money? To take revenge — to silence her — who knows? And not a lot to go on so far, but you'll find something, I know you will, Lilian.

Wyler I think I'll start by having a word with that chemist.

Charlesworth Good. And you might tell Mr Bevan that everyone can go — we'll call them in as we need them.

Wyler He won't be happy keeping the "Closed" sign on the door.

Charlesworth Oh I'm sure you'll pacify him: explain to him about scene of the crime and such like.

Wyler I think he's only interested in profit margins.

Charlesworth You're forgetting his apparent interest in the ladies.

Wyler Quite right, sir: we must never forget the ladies.

She goes through into the salon

Charlesworth stands for a moment and then takes up his hat, to stand twirling it around on his forefinger

Dance music fades up. The Lights fade

SCENE 2

The next day. Mid-morning

The Lights come up. The chairs have been moved back to their original positions. The door to Doon's office is part open. After a moment, Charlesworth comes out of the office, closes the door, and stands looking down thoughtfully, jiggling a small set of keys. Aileen comes in from downstairs. She is wearing a close-fitting silk frock and a jaunty little hat

Charlesworth Ah — Miss Wheeler — good-morning — you persuaded the constable to let you in then. (*He comes down the stairs, pocketing the keys*)

Aileen I'm surprised he's still out there.

Charlesworth I kept him there for you: knowing your penchant for "the boys in blue." (*He smiles*) I understand that you have something to tell me.

A moment. She moves to perch on the edge of the desk, taking out a cigarette. He lights it for her. She cups his hand "à la mode". She blows out smoke

Aileen I remembered something. It's probably nothing but I thought you should know.

Charlesworth waits

You asked me if Doon could have killed herself and I said no.

Charlesworth Because she had "too much life in her".

Aileen Yes. The thing is ... last night ... I couldn't stop thinking about her and I remembered ... well ... a couple of times I caught her off-guard, when she was on her own ... and she was kind of — staring ahead and hugging herself — (*she indicates*) — as though she was really frightened.

Charlesworth Frightened?

Aileen Like a little girl in a dark room. (*She dwells on the thought for a moment and then stands, looking around for an ashtray*) Well as I say it's probably nothing and I only popped in on my way to Fenwick's — they've got some rather nice frocks in their sale.

Charlesworth takes up an ashtray, takes the cigarette from her and stubs it out

Charlesworth Would you think it presumptuous if I said I think you're not at all what you want people to think you are?

Aileen Totally presumptuous. (*But*) In what way?

Charlesworth I think a lot more goes on in that head of yours than you're prepared to admit.

Aileen Oh I hope not.

Charlesworth You see? (*He smiles*)

Aileen Well as I say, I've got some shopping to do.

Charlesworth Thank you for stopping by.

Aileen Unless you'd like to come with me. I might even let you take me to lunch.

Charlesworth Some other time perhaps.

Aileen gives him her smile and makes to go out, but stops

Aileen My father was gassed in the trenches and hasn't had a day's work since. My mother runs around tables all day and comes home with ankles like balloons. My brother's in Spain risking his neck for a cause he's not even sure of any more. One night — I was still at school — and he's sitting there, my father, reading his pamphlets and spouting his socialism and I suddenly got angry and I said "where's it ever got you, this socialism? There's them and there's us, and there always will be and all the rest of it's so much twaddle to keep us in our place. Well, they're not going to keep me." I've never seen him so hurt. But I really believed it. So I saved up and got myself elocution lessons like Jessie bloody Matthews and read all the right magazines and here I am. A total fraud. A total traitor. And ashamed of myself. (*It's clear that she means it and it hurts*)

Rose comes in from downstairs, wearing a light topcoat and holding her large handbag

Rose Oh — sorry.
Aileen I keeping telling you, Macaroni ... never apologize, never explain ... (*to Charlesworth*) ... Cheery-hoh, Inspector, have a jolly good time and all that — what?

She kicks up a heel and goes out, downstairs, patting Rose's cheek as she goes

Charlesworth Good-morning, Rose, thank you for coming.
Rose That's all right.
Charlesworth D'you have to come far?
Rose No, it's just a bus — from Wandsworth.

Charlesworth indicates for her to sit down, which she does, unsure. He takes out the set of keys   Keys

Charlesworth Have you seen these before?
Rose (*too quickly*) No.
Charlesworth They belong to Miss Doon. One of them — this one — locks a drawer in her desk. I had a look in the drawer this morning. It holds a petty cash box. Opened with this key. (*He indicates another, smaller key*). There's a small amount of money in it ... some receipts ... and this ... (*He has taken a small, folded slip of paper from his pocket*) Would you like to read what it says?   small folded slip of paper
Rose (*lowering her head in shame*) I know what it says.

Charlesworth (*reading*) "I hereby admit to having taken five pounds without permission which I will pay back no later than September first." Is this your writing, Rose?
Rose No, it's Miss Doon's.
Charlesworth But this is your signature.

After a pause Rose gives a brief nod

D'you want to tell me about it?
Rose Do I have to?
Charlesworth I'm afraid you do, yes.

Wyler comes in, unseen by Rose

Charlesworth indicates for her to stay where she is. Rose works herself into the following

Rose My chap, my Eddie, is always in trouble with the bookies. I keep telling him but ... someone give him this tip for a dog, a dead certainty he said, and if Eddie had a fiver on it he could clear his debts and have enough for us to get married and that. Only he didn't have a fiver. I was in Miss Doon's office and her keys were on her desk and ... I was stupid, I know I was, but the dog was running that night and Eddie was desperate and I love him.
Charlesworth But the dead cert didn't win.
Rose Not even in the first three.
Charlesworth And Miss Doon found out.
Rose She asked me if I'd took the money and I admitted it. I only borrowed it, I said, I would have paid it back, honest I would. At first she was very nice, saying she understood and she wouldn't tell no one, but then she started to turn all nasty and made me sign this paper and kept saying she'd tell Mr Bevan and I'd get the sack and God knows what I'd do then.
Charlesworth Is that why you put the poison in her food?
Rose (*horrified*) I didn't. I didn't!
Charlesworth No. I don't think you did. (*A moment*) That's all, Rose — thank you.
Rose What am I going to do about it?
Charlesworth The money? You'll have to do what you think is right. I won't say anything about it. It's up to you.

A moment. Then Rose gives a little nod and goes out, downstairs, avoiding looking at Wyler

Charlesworth waits until she is well gone

Charlesworth Tell me about the chemist.
Wyler He confirms Mrs Gay's story. He gave her an ounce — about four teaspoons — as she said. I've also had a word with the Sussex Constabulary.
Charlesworth Interesting?
Wyler Enough to bring him in.
Charlesworth (*indicating the telephone*) Phone him now.

Wyler goes to the telephone and looks up a number in her notebook. Throughout the following, she will quietly speak into the telephone and hang up after a brief exchange

Phone notebook [handwritten marginal note]

Bevan comes in from the salon, wearing his hat

Bevan Is it really necessary to have a constable on both of the doors?
Charlesworth Good morning, Mr Bevan. Yes, I'm afraid it is. But not for much longer I hope.

cigarette case Ashtray Wastebin [handwritten marginal note]

Bevan sets down his hat and takes out his case to light himself a cigarette. Charlesworth takes up the ashtray, tips Aileen's dog-end into the waste bin and sets down the ashtray for Bevan who accepts it without thanks

Do sit down.
Bevan I'll stand, thank you.
Charlesworth As you wish. (*He smiles*) You haven't exactly told us the truth about your relationship with Miss Doon, have you, Mr Bevan?
Bevan I'm sorry, I don't know what you're talking about.
Charlesworth Then let me tell you. (*There is an unexpected coldness about him now*) The porter at the flats where you live says that she visited you there quite often.
Bevan Did he be damned.
Charlesworth This is a police enquiry, Mr Bevan: I expect people to tell me the truth. Unless they have good reason not to.
Bevan Yes, all right. We had a thing going. So what?
Charlesworth So why didn't you say?
Bevan Because I saw little point. Besides. It was all over.
Charlesworth Then why did she visit you last weekend? And why were you heard to be arguing?

A moment

Bevan She came to tell me she didn't want the job in Deauville.
Charlesworth Had you offered it to her?
Bevan More or less. And she seemed perfectly happy.

Charlesworth Did she say why she had changed her mind?

Bevan No. To be quite frank, she had been drinking and was rather — extravagant. I tried to make her change her mind but she wasn't having any. She said ... she didn't have the time. Whatever that meant. As I say, she'd been drinking.

Charlesworth Why were you so keen on her taking the job?

Bevan Because she was the best suited. And yes — all right — she could be difficult and it was a way of distancing myself from her and hoping she'd turn her rather peculiar affections elsewhere.

Charlesworth And so Miss Gregory was your second choice.

Bevan Yes. Not that she knows that and I'd rather she never does.

Charlesworth Did she know of your — private relationship with Miss Doon?

Bevan I don't broadcast these things, Inspector.

Charlesworth Bully for you.

Bevan Besides, I see little point in crossing my wires. Yes, I was also seeing Zelda — Miss Gregory — as I've no doubt George — the porter — has told you.

Charlesworth What a dangerous business you run, Mr Bevan.

Bevan There are admittedly advantages in having your women beholden to you for their bread and butter. It's tricky, of course, but it can be the spice of life, wouldn't you say?

Charlesworth No, I don't think I would, Mr Bevan.

Rachel appears at the downstairs door

Rachel Oh, I'm so sorry.

Charlesworth Not at all, Mrs Gay — in fact you've arrived at precisely the right moment. Please sit down.

She does so, concerned at the presence of Bevan

Was one of your wires Mrs Gay? (*To her*) Do excuse me — please. (*To him*) Mr Bevan?

Bevan No, she was not.

Charlesworth Then why did she on more than one occasion visit you in your apartment? Yes, the porter again.

Rachel (*to Bevan, fearfully*) What have you said?

Bevan I've said nothing, Rachel.

Charlesworth Perhaps you'd like to tell us, Mrs Gay?

She looks at him

(*Gently*) You'll have to sooner or later, you know.

Rachel (*after a pause*) When my husband started behaving so badly, I was desperately unhappy. One day I broke down and Mr Bevan asked me to go to dinner with him. To — to cheer me up.

Wyler (*flatly*) Cheer you up.

Rachel Nothing untoward happened, I swear.

Wyler (*sarcastically*) Yes, I can't see a gentleman like Mr Bevan taking advantage of a vulnerable woman.

Bevan You know, Sergeant ... even the worst of us occasionally does something decent — hard though it is to believe.

Charlesworth It was just the one occasion then.

Bevan No — twice I think. Yes, twice.

Rachel Months ago.

Charlesworth Then why did you visit Mr Bevan the night before Miss Doon died?

Bevan (*to Rachel*) I didn't know that.

Charlesworth Mrs Gay?

A moment

Rachel My husband seems determined to make our divorce as difficult as possible. He'd been asking questions about my — my behaviour. If he found out about Mr Bevan he would have done his best to make something ugly out of it. I panicked — I admit I'm inclined to over-react to things — and went round to Mr Bevan's apartment to find out if he'd said anything to anyone. Anyone. (*To Bevan*) But you weren't there.

Bevan I'm so sorry, Rachel. For — putting you in this position.

Rachel No. You were kind and I was foolish.

Charlesworth *Had* you told anyone, Mr Bevan?

Bevan As I said ... even I can do the decent thing on occasions.

Wyler And keep your wires uncrossed.

A moment

Charlesworth Thank you. Both of you. Perhaps you should take Mrs Gay for a coffee, Mr Bevan.

Bevan Yes, perhaps I should. Rachel? (*He indicates "please come with me"*)

She gives him a little smile and he escorts her into the salon, collecting his hat on the way

Wyler My grandmother used to say when a man and a woman are alone, the devil makes three.

Charlesworth Did she indeed.
Wyler Mind you, in her case the devil must have been working overtime.
She had eight kids and very rosy cheeks.

Dorian appears at the downstairs door

Dorian You wanted to see me.
Charlesworth Yes, indeed we did, Mr Pouvier. Thank you for coming
so promptly.
Dorian Yes, well, I'm only in Park Street — as I'm sure you know.

Hankie

*Charlesworth indicates for Dorian to sit down. Which he does, mopping
his brow with his pocket handkerchief*

Charlesworth Yes, it is warm, isn't it? (*He smiles, aware that it's nerves
not temperature*) Sergeant Wyler here is a very efficient woman.
Dorian I'm glad to hear it.
Charlesworth The thing being, as one of the first women to join the
Criminal Investigation Department she has to keep well abreast of her
colleagues, if not one step ahead.
Dorian Yes, well, I'm sure you haven't brought me here to take me
through Sergeant Wyler's curriculum vitae, impressive though I'm
sure it is.
Charlesworth The point being, Mr Pouvier, that Sergeant Wyler picks
up on things that others of us might be inclined to — pass by.
Dorian Oh yes?
Charlesworth The difference between Greenwich Village and Brighton,
for example. Or the connection, perhaps.

This freezes the smugness on Dorian's face. Charlesworth nods to Wyler

Wyler I've been checking back through copies of the *Brighton Argus*,
Mr Pouvier. (*She refers to her notebook*) On July the seventh of this
year, a Mr Derek Prout was fined two guineas and bound over on a
charge of indecent behaviour in a public place.

A moment

Dorian It was not ... as it appeared.
Charlesworth But Miss Doon somehow found out about it.
Dorian Nothing can ever be kept hidden, can it? It always finds its way
out of the muck. (*He takes a deep breath*) She was staying in Hove
with a friend. Of course, as fate always has it, it was the weekend they

published their wretched story. She knew my real name through the company books. She never said anything outright, just ... jab jab jab. But sometimes ... sometimes ... (*He looks at them directly*) I wanted to kill her. (*And now that he's got it off his chest, he reverts to type*) There: isn't that what you wanted to hear?

Charlesworth (*smiling*) Thank you, Mr Pouvier

Dorian Oh I can go, can I? Back to my twilight little world. It will all change, you know: one day it will all change. (*He makes to go. To Wyler*) Next time you're choosing your wardrobe, do let me help you. If nothing else, I can get it for you wholesale.

And he prances out, downstairs, as though determined to be more "gay" than ever

Wyler Not much of a life, I would have thought. Underneath all the bravado. And not much of a motive, either.

Charlesworth Whatever, I'm convinced this killing was a spur of the moment thing. Something that had built up and then... bang. D'you remember that case in Liverpool? Wallace I think his name was. Married to a woman who nagged him senseless every day for twenty three years and all he said was yes, dear, no, dear, quite so dear, and then, one day, quite out of the blue, he took up the coal hammer and caved her head in. Let me buy you a sandwich, Lilian.

Wyler As long as it doesn't poison me.

Charlesworth Did I tell you about the Irish chap? Bought himself a sandwich and is about to eat it when he sees two electrical wires hanging out of it. So he ~~dials nine-nine-nine~~ and says "I tink I've got a bomb in my sandwich. And the copper says "is it ticking?" And the Irishman says, "No, it's cheese and onion".

Wyler That's terrible.

Charlesworth I thought it was rather good ...

They go out through the salon doors

Music. The Lights fade

<h2 align="center">Scene 3</h2>

The next day. Late morning

Gregory sits, but can't keep still and gets up to pace. She sees something she doesn't like, something a little out of place and irritably, unnecessarily, tidies it

Charlesworth comes in from the salon

Charlesworth Miss Gregory ... good-morning.
Gregory (*stiffly*) Good-morning.

He moves further into the room, setting his hat aside

Charlesworth Oh and before I forget — I met someone last night — quite coincidentally — who is a client of yours.
Gregory (*still stiff*) Oh yes?
Charlesworth Fiancée of an old chum of mine — Delia Blakiston.
Gregory Miss Blakiston — yes.
Charlesworth Singing your praises to high heaven.
Gregory How very gratifying.

Charlesworth smiles

Charlesworth So then: Sergeant Wyler tells me there's something you want to talk to me about — in confidence.
Gregory Yes.
Charlesworth I was rather hoping that might be the case. (*He again smiles, indicating for her to sit*)

She chooses not to

Gregory The thing is ... and this is very hard for me to say ... the thing is ... I suddenly realized ...

Wyler comes through from the salon

Wyler Everyone's here now, Inspector: would you like to see them one at a time or all together?
Charlesworth All together please.
Wyler (*towards the salon*) Would you like to come through, please?

Wyler remains holding the door open as the others come through. Rose carries her large handbag

Charlesworth I think, Miss Gregory, that I know what you were going to say — in fact, I've been waiting for you to say it.
Aileen (*singing*) Here we are, here we are, here we are again!
Irene Aileen — shush!
Charlesworth Will you all sit down, please?

They do so, some moving the chairs or stools

Miss Macinerny — I wonder if you'd mind sitting here?

Rose was about to sit near Gregory, but he indicates a place away from her. She sits there, unsure of his intentions. Some people smoke, sharing ashtrays

Charlesworth Good-morning — once again. I won't keep you long — I hope — and I think I can assure you that this will be the last of such — gatherings.
Bevan Thank God for that.

Charlesworth leaves it long enough for Bevan to feel awkward at his remark, before

Charlesworth We've talked about the possibility of accident or suicide but I'm now convinced that Miss Doon was murdered.

Varying reaction from them ... Rachel's hand goes to her mouth, Bevan offers "absurd" etc.

Dorian Are you saying someone in this room killed her?
Charlesworth Yes, Mr Pouvier. Someone in this room killed her.

This brings a more subdued response

Miss Doon was murdered. It was not premeditated but was, if you like, a crime of convenience. It was also a crime committed in error because the intended victim was not Miss Doon but Miss Gregory.

Reaction from the others

Bevan What do you mean — Miss Gregory?
Charlesworth Shall you say it or shall I, Miss Gregory?

A moment

Gregory She didn't order any food. But I did.
Rachel Of course!
Charlesworth That is right, isn't it, Rose? Miss Doon was given Miss Gregory's food?

Rose works it out and gives a little nod

Bevan How can you be sure of that? There wasn't just the one plate, for God's sake — they didn't have *numbers* on them.

Charlesworth No — but Miss Gregory was the only one who had ordered rice. Isn't that right, Rose?

Rose Yes. And besides, all the others had been taken.

The others look at each other, realizing that this was indeed what had happened

Charlesworth Whose idea was it that Miss Doon should be offered Miss Gregory's food?

Irene Mine.

Rachel Are you sure, Rene, I thought it was me.

Irene No. No. It was definitely me. I told Rose to ask her, anyway.

Bevan Does it really matter?

Wyler It might matter a great deal, Mr Bevan.

Charlesworth So. You offered Miss Doon the food and she accepted.

Rose Yes. Except she said she didn't want no pudding. (*Generally*) She wasn't a one for puddings, was she? (*Back to Charlesworth*) Anyway, just as well because there wasn't any.

Bevan (*irritably*) Why would anyone want to kill Miss Gregory?

Aileen (*sotto voce to Irene*) Is he kidding?

Irene giggles almost hysterically. All this is far too much for her

Irene Sorry.

Charlesworth As I've said, this is a murder that wasn't planned. Something happened here that morning that pushed someone over the edge. The final straw on the camel's back, you might say. So we're looking for something out of the ordinary.

Bevan (*tersely*) Like what?

Charlesworth Like the announcement of who was to be sent to your new branch in Deauville.

Bevan Are you saying someone wanted to kill Zelda — Miss Gregory — to stop her getting the job? Ridiculous.

Dorian There were only two people in the running, anyway.

Irene Miss Doon and Miss Gregory.

Aileen So if Doon wanted Gregory out of the way, she'd hardly take the stuff herself, would she?

Charlesworth But it was Miss Doon who was offered the job. Not Miss Gregory.

Gregory (*stiffly*) That isn't true.

Bevan I'm afraid it is, Zelda. She agreed and then changed her mind. Which is why ——

Gregory Yes. Thank you, I understand.

Charlesworth nods to Wyler

Wyler Miss Gregory, you said you saw Miss Macinerny get rid of the crystals.
Gregory Yes.
Wyler You actually stood over her.
Gregory Yes.
Wyler Why? Because you didn't trust her?
Gregory Yes, frankly.
Wyler What did she do?
Gregory I don't follow you.
Wyler With the crystals. Did she tip them out of the paper or just throw the whole lot in?
Rose Excuse me.
Charlesworth One moment, Rose.
Gregory I'm not sure that I remember.
Wyler Try.
Gregory She ... just threw the bag in and flushed it away.
Charlesworth You're sure of that, are you?
Gregory Yes.
Charlesworth Because Rose says she tipped the crystals out of the paper first.
Gregory Then she's quite wrong. She forgets everything. Ask anyone. Besides, is it really important to know if —
Charlesworth Are you trying to protect her, Miss Gregory?
Gregory How do you mean "protect her"?
Charlesworth I mean precisely that.
Gregory I'm trying neither to protect nor to implicate. I'm simply telling you the truth.
Charlesworth Which means that you lied, Rose.
Gregory She didn't lie, she made a mistake.
Charlesworth You lied, didn't you Rose?
Gregory Please leave her alone.
Aileen Yes — leave her alone. She forgets things. So what?
Charlesworth What exactly did you forget, Rose?
Rose Nothing.
Charlesworth (*very firm and cold*) What exactly did you forget?

A moment

Rose I had my hands full when I went downstairs, so I put the little bag in my pocket, my apron pocket. And I forgot it was there.

Charlesworth So you *didn't* throw it away.
Rose Yes I did! Only ... only not straight away.

Charles waits for her to continue. She doesn't

Charlesworth Go on.
Rose Please, I ——
Charlesworth Go on, Rose.
Rose Just after the boy come with the dinners, I went to use my handkerchief and found I still had the little bag. Miss Gregory come downstairs and saw me with it. She got really angry and said get rid of it right away ... give it here, she said, you can't be trusted to do *anything*.

Wyler somewhat pointedly clears her throat

Charlesworth (*smiling*) Thank you, Sergeant, point taken. (*But*) Why didn't you tell me this before, Rose?
Aileen (*flatly*) She forgot.
Rose I would have done but Miss Gregory said it would look bad for me and apart from anything else, I could lose my job.
Charlesworth So you *were* trying to protect her, Miss Gregory.

Gregory gives a tight-lipped little movement of the hand

What time did this happen?
Gregory I've no idea.
Charlesworth (*to Rose*) But it was after the food was delivered.
Rose Sorry?
Gregory She's already said.
Charlesworth And put into the hot cupboards in the kitchen.
Rose Yes.
Charlesworth And it was *still* in the hot cupboards.
Rose Yes. I mean no.
Charlesworth Which is it, Rose?
Rose Well most people had already taken theirs — in fact they all had. Except Miss Gregory because she wasn't staying, anyway.
Charlesworth So that the only food left downstairs was that originally intended for Miss Gregory.
Rose Yes.
Charlesworth Was it before or after this that the food was offered to Miss Doon?
Rose I don't remember.
Charlesworth Miss Gregory?

Gregory I've no idea.
Irene It was afterwards.
Rose (*with no real recollection*) Yes, afterwards.
Irene I called down the stairs for her to go up and see if Miss Doon wanted to eat anything.
Rose That's right, isn't it, Miss Gregory? You was with me.
Charlesworth Is it, Miss Gregory?
Gregory Probably.
Rose (*to Gregory*) Yes, you said for me not to just stand there but do what I was told.
Gregory (*to Charlesworth*) Yes, she's quite right. That's what happened.
Charlesworth Thank you.
Rachel Excuse me ... I've just thought of something.
Charlesworth Yes, Mrs Gay?
Rachel What I was going to say was ... if someone intended to kill Miss Gregory, why would they allow her food to be given to Miss Doon — why wouldn't they try to stop it?
Charlesworth Precisely, Mrs Gay. Precisely. (*He spreads his hands as if to say "now you see what this has been leading to"*) And the answer we now know is that either there wasn't enough time or the opportunity to stop the food being served or that Miss Gregory was never the intended victim — that the poison was indeed meant for Miss Doon.
Bevan (*irritably*) Well then — which was it?
Charlesworth Sergeant?
Wyler (*referring to her notes*) Miss Macinerny ... you said ... "Just after the boy come with the dinners, I went to use my handkerchief and found I still had the little bag. Miss Gregory come downstairs and saw me with it. She got really angry and said get rid of it right away... give it here, she said, you can't be trusted to do *anything*." (*She closes her notebook*) "Give it here, she said."
Charlesworth And did you "give it here", Rose?
Rose I can't remember.
Charlesworth (*slowly*) Did you give the bag to Miss Gregory?
Rose I can't ——
Charlesworth Did you give the ——
Rose Yes! Yes!
Charlesworth Thank you.

The others begin to turn their eyes to Gregory who sits looking straight ahead

Charlesworth You see, Miss Gregory, by trying to deflect suspicion away from yourself, you did precisely the opposite. You inadvertently raised the question to which the only answer is that Miss Doon died because you intended to kill her.

Gregory No! (*She brings herself to order*) I did not intend to kill her. I did not intend to kill her.

Bevan Good God.

Gregory Good God nothing! It was you — you — who forced me into it — you with your promises — lies, all lies — you just used me like you use every woman stupid enough to believe you. Well to hell with you — to hell with all of you. I know what you all think of me — well let me tell you, I've given my life to this place — he knew *nothing* when his father died — *nothing*.

Bevan (*gently*) Zelda ... I don't think you should say anymore until ——

Gregory After all he said he suddenly announced that he was sending me to Deauville. I know what he was really after — not him, the both of them — he and Doon — they wanted me out of the way ——

Bevan Zelda ——

Gregory Don't deny it, don't you dare try to deny it!

She looks like she might strike him and Wyler makes a move but Charlesworth motions for her to stay where she is

Charlesworth And so you killed Miss Doon, not because you wanted to go to France, but because you didn't.

Gregory I didn't mean to kill her, I tell you. I was so angry. So — hurt. When the girl went upstairs to see if Doon wanted my food I realized I still had the crystals in my hand. I put some — not all of it, not all of it — into the food and — got rid of the rest. I only wanted to make her ill. I thought, if she was ill he wouldn't dare send me to France because no one else was capable of looking after this place — and they wouldn't be, they wouldn't be. (*Then, as though all the strength has gone from her*). I didn't want to kill her, I really didn't want to kill her.

A moment

Charlesworth Take Miss Gregory to the car, will you, Sergeant?

Wyler (*not forcefully*) This way, please. (*She indicates for Gregory to go downstairs. She moves to the doorway*)

Gregory Well you'll all be very happy with yourselves, won't you? You've finally got rid of me.

She attempts a haughty smile and goes downstairs, followed by Wyler

A moment

Irene How could she have ... killed someone?

Charlesworth I think she was telling the truth — I don't think she meant to. And I think Miss Doon would have lived — although not for much longer.

Bevan How d'you mean, not for much longer?

Charlesworth She'd been ill for some time. There were letters and prescriptions in her flat. I spoke to her doctor. In simple terms, she had a condition that would ultimately lead to kidney failure and so to her death. The last time he saw her was Friday evening when he told her there was nothing that could be done for her. That was why she must have changed her mind, Mr Bevan.

Bevan But good God why didn't she say?

Aileen Because the last thing she would have wanted was our pity.

Rachel Yes — yes, you're right.

Dorian (*more to himself*) I wish I'd known. I really wish I'd known.

Charlesworth Well — thank you, everyone. And tomorrow you can resume business, Mr Bevan.

Bevan Of a kind, Inspector ... of a kind.

He nods generally and goes out. The others follow him, apart from Aileen and Charlesworth

Aileen Will she be hanged?

Charlesworth I don't think so. Not with a half-decent lawyer.

Aileen But she'll go to prison.

Charlesworth For a couple of years, perhaps.

Aileen Two years. That's what — nineteen thirty-nine — September nineteen thirty-nine. I wonder what the rest of us will be doing?

Charlesworth (*smiling*) You'll be mistress of some vast stately mansion, won't you?

Aileen Either that or on a protest march. In the meantime, why don't you take me to the flicks?

Charlesworth What I can do is take you for a cup of tea so that we can talk about it.

They start to move towards the salon. Charlesworth takes up his hat

Aileen D'you like William Powell?

Charlesworth I prefer Myrna Loy.

Aileen There's a new *Thin Man* playing.
Charlesworth Ah! Nick and Nora — I love them.
Aileen Not as much as I do — I can even quote their lines.
Charlesworth (*doing his William Powell impersonation*) "Oh that's all right Joe, it's *my* dog. Oh, and this is my wife."
Aileen (*doing her Myrna Loy*) "Excuse me ... may I have a word with you about the billing?"

Charlesworth opens the salon door for her and she goes out

He is about to follow her when Rose hurries in from downstairs

Rose Sorry — I forgot my bag.
Charlesworth Oh.

He smiles and goes out

She stands, trying to remember where she was sitting. She remembers and goes to the chair. And finds the bag

She holds it up triumphantly to the audience, and hurries out, down the stairs

As she goes, music plays

CURTAIN

FURNITURE AND PROPERTY LIST

ACT I

SCENE 1

On stage: A few black and chrome chairs
Three black and chrome stools
Cutting table
Small desk. *On it*: pen, telephone, pile of mail ~~Typewriter~~
Ashtray
Waste bin
Full-length mirror
Dress and hat display stands
Red frock (on one of the display stands)
Shelves. *On them*: material samples
Small selection of shoes
Handbag (for **Irene**)

Off stage: Duster (**Mac**)
Handbag (**Gregory**)
Grey evening dress (**Irene**)
Panama hat, folded *News Chronicle* newspaper (**Rachel**)
Pins (**Dorian**)
Cover for dress (**Mac**)
Glass of water (**Mac**)
Small paper bag, twisted closed (**Rachel**)
Toothbrush (**Rachel**)
Dresses (**Irene**)
Tray holding a coffee cup, milk jug etc. (**Mac**)
Ten shilling note (**Doon**)
Packet of cigarettes, coins (**Mac**)
Order book (**Irene**) *p 2 3* .
Tray (**Irene**)

Personal: **Bevan**: silver cigarette case containing cigarettes
Doon: cigarette and lighter
Dorian: wristwatch

SCENE 2

Set: Jug of water
               Glasses
               Plates

Off stage: Tray (**Mac**)
               Handbag (**Gregory**)
               Biscuit, mug of coffee (**Aileen**)

Personal: **Dorian**: coloured handkerchief, watch
               Gregory: gloves

ACT II

SCENE 1

Strike: Newspaper, mug of coffee

Set: Rearrange chairs and stools

Personal: **Rachel**: cigarette, handkerchief
               Bevan: cigarette
               Wyler   note book

SCENE 2

Set: Rearrange chairs and stools

Off stage: Small set of keys (**Charles**)
               Large handbag (**Mac**)

Personal: **Aileen**: cigarette
               Charles: cigarette lighter, folded piece of paper (in pocket)
               Bevan: silver cigarette case containing cigarettes, lighter
               Dorian: pocket handkerchief

SCENE 3

Off stage: Large handbag (**Mac**)

LIGHTING PLOT

Practical fittings required: light that flashes by the door to the salon

One interior, the same throughout

ACT I, SCENE 1

To open: General interior lighting

Cue 1	**Irene**: "— see how it goes." *Light by door flashes*	(Page 19)
Cue 2	**Irene** comes down from **Doon**'s office *Light by door flashes*	(Page 26)
Cue 3	**Irene** goes downstairs *Lights fade*	(Page 28)

ACT I, SCENE 2

To open: General interior lighting

No cues

ACT II, SCENE 1

To open: General interior lighting

Cue 4	Dance music fades up *Lights fade*	(Page 55)

ACT II, SCENE 2

To open: General interior lighting

Cue 5	Music plays *Lights fade*	(Page 63)

ACT II, SCENE 3

To open: General interior lighting

No cues

EFFECTS PLOT

ACT I

ACT II

USE OF COPYRIGHT MUSIC

A licence issued by Samuel French Ltd to perform this play does not include permission to use the Incidental music specified in this copy. Where the place of performance is already licensed by the PERFORMING RIGHT SOCIETY a return of the music used must be made to them. If the place of performance is not so licensed then application should be made to the Performing Right Society, 29 Berners Street, London W1T 3AB (website: www.mcps-prs-alliance.co.uk).

A separate and additional licence from PHONOGRAPHIC PERFORMANCE LTD, 1 Upper James Street, London W1F 9DE (website: www.ppluk.com) is needed whenever commercial recordings are used.